JAGUAR vs. PORSCHE

THE BATTLE FOR LE MANS

1987

BY KEN WELLS
PHOTOGRAPHY: DAVE CUNDY, KEN WELLS

CONTENTS

Published by	William Kimberley Limited 4 Church Close London N20 0JU
First Published	September 1987
Copyright	Kewkar Racing and William Kimberley Limited
Printed by	The Lavenham Press Limited
Written by	Ken Wells David Cundy
Edited by	Soheila Ilbagian
Photographers	David Cundy Ken Wells
Special Thanks to	Derek Hetherington of Leitz Instruments Alan Geisler & Anne Mapson of Fuji Roger Elson & Steve Gibbs The press offices of Silverstone & Brands Hatch Martin Whittaker of the RACMSA M. Jean Marc Desnues of the A.C.O. All at O.S.C.A.R.
Special Note	Copies of most of the photographs herein – and many more besides – are available from:– Kewkar Racing, 4 Highfield Rise, Althorne, Essex CM3 6DN, England. Please enclose a stamped, addressed envelope with any enquiry. Thank you.
Overseas Distributors	Motorbooks International, P.O. Box 2, 729 Prospect Ave., Osceola, Wisconsin 54020, U.S.A.

ISBN 0 946132 43 7

'BLUE SKYS', PURPLE HAZE

In the bleak mid-winter when days were short and snow was deep, young men's thoughts turned to such things as cloudless horizons, crimson sunsets and oh! oh! oh! those summer nights – tell me more, tell me more . . .

Mine, on the other hand, were about the Sarthe and soccer – in a word, Coventry. With both the Racing Car Show and third round of the F.A. Cup imminent an overactive imagination thought the unthinkable: could that famous city take both honours? Victoire au Mans and Up For T'Cup? What a double! What a pair!

What a wally! (Apologies to David Bailey.) The aberration was but brief, the cold light of day as harsh as an icy stare from 'her indoors', reality dawning to consider F.C. had won nowt in a century of trying and S.C. only a solitary success despite all their endeavours, even that being a home match. Why should City choose this of all years to overcome the Uniteds, the Liverpools, the Tottenhams? How could T.W.R. take on the almighty Porsche at their French proving ground, a race where only one car wearing a Jag flag had even finished in nigh on a quarter century? Nah, no chance. Where's the snow shovel . . .

The only spades Jaguar took to Spain were the aces up their sleeves in the form of their latest trump cards, XJR-8s for a new driving force of Cheever/Boesel and Watson/Lammers, last year's cars being comprehensively revised by Tony Southgate to warrant new designations. The changes were in detail, suspension and fuel system amongst them, a whopping great seven litre motor beating at their heart so joining an illustrious club featuring Ford Mk IV and Chaparral, the whole package topped by a new livery with less diamond white, more green, orange and purple. It is supposed to make them even more noticeable – is that possible?

They took the hopes of millions who sought an end to 'Champions' being a Deutsche anagram for 'Stuttgart' or 'Porsche AG'. They returned with two wins!

This year Group C had forsaken its traditional Monza opener for Madrid, round one possibly billed as a 'Drama in Jarama', a 360 kms sprint race followed a week later by an arbitrary 1000 kms enduro in Jerez. It actually became a Six Hours by dint of a 'Maximum Time' rule etched in plaster by Paris, a genuine FISA cop-out clause supposedly aimed more at Donald Duck weather than Mickey Mouse circuits.

Whatever, T.W.R. had their measure with Jan and John winning first time out after the sister car was delayed, Eddie and Raul following up their third with a storybook victory in Jerez where 'Wattie' decanted the XJR-8 with a broken driveshaft early on. The Jaguars even had the temerity to claim pole position at Jarama, Eddie's endeavours ably supported by Lammers' hammers to nail second slot as well.

RIGHT: It was the Jaguars that set the pace in the races up to Le Mans.

It was the first time pole had gone to a non-turbo car – quite an echeeverment!

Heading the entry list had been three 962Cs from reigning Teams' champions Brun Motorsport, their familiar liveries hiding the fact that one was a new chassis from John Thompson's outfit and featured carbon fibre where aluminium used to be. Kremer, with two cars present, had also been a TCP customer although less adventurous in specification – more gargle, less gamble. Between these two teams they featured such familiar names as Brancatelli, Jelinski, Larrauri and de Villota, but it was left to Kremer protégés Kris Nissen and Volker Weidner to achieve best, fourth then second to prove the old adage that in order to finish first (or thereabouts) first you had to finish.

Fastest of the Porsche privateers was the latest creation from GTi although it could only manage eighth at Jarama, waiting on the line with a shredded tyre as Watson reeled off his final laps, Palmer having lost not only sixth position but house points by unnecessarily baulking the leader's progress earlier on. Returning to Group C after a sabbatical good Doctor Jonathan was now teamed with the underrated Mauro Baldi, the equipe fronted by Richard Lloyd now renamed Britten Lloyd Racing in deference to his partner, as if complimenting their restyled masterpiece with its easily recognisable low rear bodywork and centrally mounted wing. Some pundits suggested they should have the *Courage* to rename it, such are the non-German influences in its concept.

The World Endurance Champion Derek Bell again partnered Hans Stuck to undertake a full campaign with Mass and Wollek joining at Jerez, the team coming out to play more often than the once intended. Since Fuji '86 much midnight oil had been burned in the Land of Bad Württemberg, notably with regards to the troublesome and heavy double-clutch PDK transmission, the factory cars now down to the weight limit of 850 kgs. They approached the season with optimism despite stories of excellent Jaguar testing performances

already rife, knowing many had flattered only to deceive.

With an all Silk Cut front row at round one it was almost a case of who was fooling whom, Hanschen a ciggy paper back in third well clear of Baldi et al. Once bitten twice shy, there would be no repeat of this lapse, Porsche 17 claiming top slot at every other event in the build up for Le Mans.

Racing was a different matter, the Rothmans Porsche actually leading both Spanish events, but unable to maintain the pressure. At Jarama, King Derek lost out to 'Wattie' in their private Battle of Bognor, the Purple Knight, seeing a chink in his neighbour's armour at the hairpin, was through and away. A gap which grew to a dozen seconds finally reduced to a couple come the flag, John adamant he was pacing himself, 'Dinger' not so sure.

Jaguar let them have another one at Jerez, Wollek/Mass pulling out a one lap advantage after four hours only to see their hopes shattered with their

1

gearbox. Their sister car, Silk Cut 5, was there, however, to pick up the pieces. Meanwhile the BEST 962C, delayed by turbo and PDK difficulties, managed to salvage third place in a race of attrition, where fourth and fifth places went to cars from the C2 class.

In relative terms Spain was a calamity for the Porsche platoons, a triumph for Tom's Terrors, the results an excellent fillip to the championship. Not only in this Sceptred Isle did race fans welcome a genuine challenge to Porsche supremacy, everywhere enthusi-asts rejoiced at a prospect of breaking the Deutsche dictatorship.

It was two weeks until Monza and a full 1000 kms, a fortnight for Stuttgart to redress the balance as key personnel spoke of revenge: 'it's the worst thing Jag could have done, winning those first two races . . .'.

Also aimed against T.W.R. were the mighty Joest team, their only pre-Le Mans appearance featuring two 962Cs, the legendary 956-117 consigned to the history books, Klaus Ludwig's continued presence a link

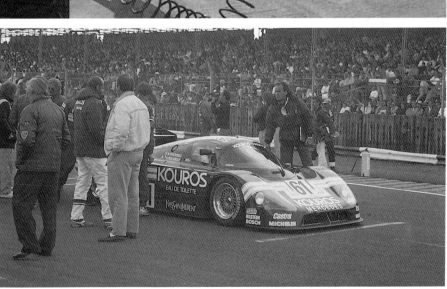

AUTOGLASS

The 24 hour service
AUTOGLASS

Autoglass are on hand, around the clock, when motorists of Britain break *any* glass in their vehicle. The service that is recommended by Motor Insurers and the AA to members, moves into top gear when drivers of cars, coaches, trucks or heavy plant dial direct free on 0800 36 36 36. A centrally controlled network of bases ensure fast and efficient service, nationwide.

Autoglass are proud of their track record – whether the glass is fitted in a base or, in an emergency, on the road by one of their fleet in the distinctive red and gold livery that is the mark of an organisation working day and night to maintain its lead in automotive glass replacement.

8

Automotive Glass Replacement Champions

The 24 Hour man ...
Derek Bell MBE

The 24 hour man, five times winner of the Le Mans 24 hour race. Winning in 1975, 1981, 1982, 1986 and in 1987 in a Porsche 962C, partnered by Hans Stuck and Al Holbert, he became the first British driver to win Le Mans five times. Le Mans — 24 hours of concentrated teamwork, attention to detail and precise rapid decisions. Organisation of the highest calibre is essential to compete in this ultimate long distance race. Derek Bell twice World Sports Car Champion has a wide range of talent as a racing driver, but he is also a team man — and as such wears the Autoglass logo proudly on his race overalls, allying himself to an organisation dedicated to all the principals of teamwork that he knows are so vital for success.

9

with an illustrious past. The future would become more circumspect, one a 'd.n.f.' and the other fourth to split Brun's best efforts, Walter B himself a very early retirement again. It is always a bit sad when you buy the ball and don't get a decent kick.

Kicking himself was Raul Boesel. Despite all the bally-hoo any threat to Silk Cut disappeared when Wollek's machine ingested some foreign matter into its turbo after about 2½ hours. Bell/Stuck were already delayed after tangling with the Liqui-Moly car where Giacomelli replaced Palmer who was competing in Rio. Up front John Neilsen sat in for Cheever, partnering Boesel in second place behind Watson/Lammers, well clear of their pursuers as the race entered its final stages, nearly home and almost dry. Then it started to rain.

Although there were only a handful of laps to go it was sufficiently hard to need grooved tyres, Lammers pitting as instructed while Raul missed his cue and sailed on before sliding off on the slippery stuff, up to his embarrassment in sand. *Merde Alors!* If it is not Jerez '86 . . . Sadly the Tom Cat was stuck in the kitty litter, happy to stay where it was. Second place passed to a grateful Bell and Stuck. To Boesel, a

former showjumper, it amounted to four faults and a refusal.

This indiscretion apart, it was another fine display by the Purple Porsche Eaters, three straights wins, no prisoners. A sprint then a couple of endurance events, one slow the other fast, had shown those XJR-8s to be highly competitive in virtually any conditions, only one more task to complete before that ultimate challenge, the 24 Hours of Le Mans.

Silverstone, the Autoglass 1000. This event gains in stature every year, now regarded by all as THE prelude to La Sarthe, a final showdown before Le Big One.

Their spiritual home, being not far from Coventry or T.W.R.'s Kidlington base, Jaguar returned as conquering heroes to the scene of that historic maiden victory twelve long months earlier. Much had happened in the interim: then they were possibles, now they are probables.

So trust Mercedes to steal some of their thunder, Stuttgart's 'other' manufacturer debuting their Kouros bedecked Sauber C9 with remarkable effect as Mike Thackwell – teamed here with Pescarolo – came within 6/100ths of knocking Hans-Joachim off pole, the sound of that 'mildly' (!)

turbocharged five litre V8 resonating across the Northamptonshire plain. Some reckoned it had nearly 1000 BHP in qualifying.

The Blue Beauty was a welcome addition of variety to CI, the only other outsider being Yves Courage's Cougar which had debuted solidly at Monza, this 956/962 engined beastie adding more ire to the fire of when is a Porsche not a Porsche. Tim Lee-Davey was supposed to have brought his latest Tiga Turbo but turned up. alone. Surely, after last year, he was not planning to enter Le Mans with an unraced car!

Thackwell led spectacularly for nearly half an hour, finally falling back onto his fuel allowance then out altogether when a misfire preceded suspension failure, having been the first car not carrying Rothmans or Silk Cut livery to lead this term.

Cheever then took control and after that it was as if the Jaguar drivers were having turns to lead, even a third Le Mans-spec. machine for Neilsen/Martin Brundle enjoying some laps of glory before engine failure sidelined it. The XJR-8LM had not expected to be 'too' competitive around Silverstone – *sans* downforce ready for the Mulsanne – but it was all too much for

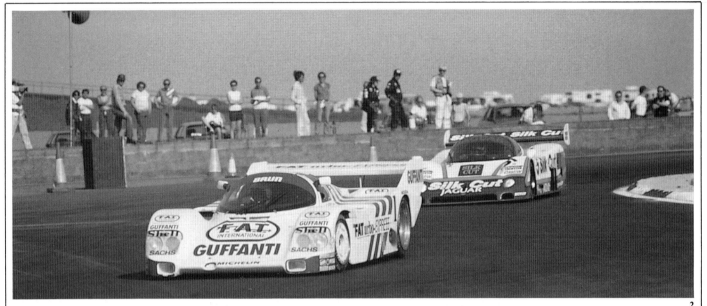

2

1. Mike Thackwell in the Sauber-Mercedes surprised everybody by leading the first 16 laps at Silverstone. 2. The Lammers/Watson Jaguar hounds the Brun/Schaeffer Porsche. 3. The Kremer team have been going through rough times since their last success at Monza 1985. 4. The Larrauri/Sigala Brun Porsche is harried by the Brundle/Nielsen Jaguar. 5. The Silverstone based BLR/Liqui Moly's version of the Porsche 962C. Overleaf: the Bell/Stuck Porsche which finished third at Silverstone.

3

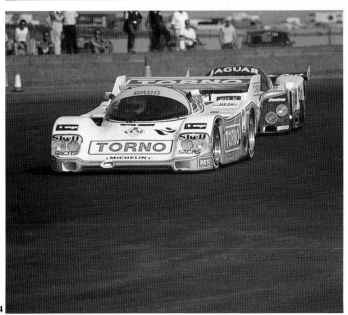

4

5

Porsche, Number 17 holding on the best it could – pre-race comments having been less bullish than Italy: 'Well it is a six years old chassis, and, well . . .' – simply unable to run at Jaguar pace. Its sister car, stricken by fuel problems, would come a poor fourth, the rest nowhere.

Taking over for their final stints all that really remained was to find out whether Lammers or Cheever would take the chequered flag. Bruno Sotty then added his twist to the tale by collecting Larrauri's Torno Porsche, ironically the same 962C which had to be rescued from the sandpit after an earlier tangle with Neilsen, Walter Brun probably now wishing it had remained there. Both his car and the Oudet Tiga were destroyed in the mayhem.

When the pace car finally completed its work there were only a dozen laps to run, Eddie sprinting clear before the HOLD boards were shown to both drivers by their pit crews. Cheever/ Boesel 2 – Watson/Lammers 2, it cannot be fairer than that.

Although Jaguar combos had won all races to date they were not clear in the title chase, Bell and Stuck only one

point adrift of Watson/Lammers with Cheever/Boesel another two further back, the Porsche pair close by virtue of being the only top team to have finished every event. And as everyone looked forward to France that was the key: Le Mans is a race for survival and Porsche are very good at that.

A week after Silverstone most major combatants assembled at Le Mans for their Test Day, the only opportunity to run at the circuit prior to race week, regular runners complemented by the likes of WM Peugeot with their latest Mulsanne-mobile, Nissan and Toyota, former World Champion Alan Jones amongst their numbers. Absentees included Cheever and Brundle, both engaged in the Belgian G.P. where the on-track spa-ring only acted as a sideshow to 'The Big Fight', Mauler Mansell taking Slogger Senna warmly by the throat for the FISA weight title. A year paired together in sportscar, would probably do the both of them a lot of good!

Meanwhile, back at the Sarthe, Raul Boesel was setting fastest overall time, his 3'24.38" no comparison to previous efforts because of a new chicane at Dunlop Curve, his 225 mph

down Mulsanne notably quicker than any Porsche although they were all outgazzed by the prima Cougar at 229, Pierre-Henri Raphanel in command for La Belle France.

So the scene was set; four weeks later they would all return to do battle proper for the greatest prize of all. To many Jaguar were outright favourites: simply a matter of extending four into five. But this is different, this is Le Mans, the most gruelling test in motorsport, the events so far only hills whereas Le Grand Prix d'Endurance is a mountain.

It would be far more open than they imagined. After all, who would really bet on a great sprinter pitted against the world's top long distance runners over a marathon?

Who would bet on Coventry City winning their first ever trophy, the 1987 F.A. Cup Final? The very same weekend as those Le Mans tests, Jaguar's home city rejoiced in its soccer victory, the 'Sky Blues' triumphing with a late flourish.

One half of the Winter's tale had come true. Was it an omen? Would Jaguar really win Le Mans? Here we go, here we go, here we go.   (KW)

1. Thackwell's Sauber-Mercedes is chased by Cheever's Jaguar in the opening laps at Silverstone. 2. The Richard Cleare March-Porsche about to be lapped by the winning Jaguar at Silverstone. 3. The works Porsche runs passes Larrauri's car which had crashed into Bruno Sotty's C2 Tiga after the Frenchman had moved into the path of the Porsche while being lapped. The Tiga ended up a sorry looking mess on the pit straight. 4. The Silverstone race was used as a test session by Tom Walkinshaw to try out the super-slippery Le Mans car (No. 6).

C2 – POSTMAN'S KNOCK

Forget C1 for providing the thrills and excitement in the World Sports Car Championship this year, the real battle for top honours is in the increasingly important C2 division of the Championship, a fight waged with great skill and increasing competitiveness between the Spice Fiero of Gordon Spice and Fermin Velez, and the Ray Mallock/David Leslie combination driving the Ecosse newly bedecked in the bright red and yellow livery of Swiftair. If variety is the spice of life, then Gordon's Spice is without doubt the variety of machine needed to win the C2 championship this year, Gordon and Fermin taking the chequered flag on three out of four occasions and finishing in a close second place to the Ecosse the other time, while the Ecosse team, based in Northamptonshire, had to settle for the runner-up position in the other three races of the championship. There may be faster machines in C2 than the Spice and Ecosse but the answer to their success seems to be the immaculate standard of preparation they both achieve, the cars always looking as though they have just been driven from the showroom, a quick flick of a duster and ready to go.

Round one of the championship was a Supersprint of some 224.3 miles held in bright sunshine on the tight Jarama circuit which lies about twenty miles north of the Spanish capital, Madrid. A Jaguar was on pole, but an unfamiliar name took the C2 pole, the vastly underrated and very talented Will Hoy, co-driving with Martin Schanche in the brand new Lucky Strike sponsored Argo-Zakspeed Turbo JM20. They set a time on race tyres (no qualifiers from Goodyear) of 1 minute 21.22 seconds almost 1½ seconds clear of the next C2 machine which was inevitably the Spice/Velez combination in the Spice-Cosworth SF86 now in the white and blue Danone colours. Another new car sat in the third spot on the grid, the turbocharged Tiga-Ford BDT-E GC287 of Thorkild Thyrring and Leif Lindstrom with a time of 1 minute 24.90 seconds.

The rest of the C2 entry in the race consisted of the Mallock/Leslie Ecosse once again with Cosworth power, Mike Wilds and Ian Harrower in the ageing but still effective ADA Gebhardt-Cosworth 843, Ruedi Seher and Hellmut Mundas in the even older URD Junior Team/Kenwood URD-BMW C81, Costas Los and Pasquale Barbiero in the Cosmik RBR/Metaxa Tiga-Cosworth GC286 and finally the Charles Ivey entered Turbo Tiga-Porsche GC 287. The Techno Alba-Cosworth AR3 which was to have been driven by Jean Pierre Frey and Luigi Taverna was sidelined before the start with engine problems after posting a time in practice 4/100ths quicker than the Ecosse.

When the flag dropped it was Velez who got the drop on the rest of the field to take an early lead harried relentlessly by Thyrring, Hoy and Wilds who were soon to be joined by

Leslie, the Ecosse having spent the first laps of the race bottled up behind Seher in the URD, a handful in corners but still very fast in a straight line. Battle was joined with some ferocity by the leaders, Thyrring hitting the front for a few of the early laps before Velez took the lead back again. The pace was too hot to last, first to drop back was Hoy with fuel read-out problems, his computer having gone walkabout. Velez had the same problem but decided he could live with it and gradually increased his lead before handing the car over to Gordie with sufficient lead for him to stroke the car home to an easy win. With Spice firmly established in first place, the drama was taking place behind him, Thyrring putting the Tiga BDT-E in second spot only to be hauled in by the near brakeless Ecosse towards the end of the race when the Tiga ran short of fuel. The Tiga just held on to third, however, because Harrower in the Gebhardt found himself with gear selection bothers, the gap to the Tiga being only 5 seconds at the finish. The only other car to finish was the URD which was fifth in class and 17 laps down on Velez/Spice, but plugging away gamely.

Of the retirements Martin Schanche was the unluckiest, his Argo being effectively destroyed when Kris Nissen in the Kremer Porsche punted the Argo off the track ending its race against the barriers. The Cosmik Tiga stopped on lap 81 with fuel problems, and the Ivey Tiga-Porsche was out on lap 4 with engine problems.

One week later the teams assembled at Jerez in southern Spain to recommence battle in the first of the year's 1000 kilometre races. The entry was much the same as at Jarama but the Ivey Tiga-Porsche had retired hurt back to base. The entry list, however, was swollen by the inclusion of the ALD-BMW of Dominique Lacaud/ Gerard Tremblay/Louis Descartes, Kelmar Racing's Tiga, the ex-Spice championship winning car and the Bardon of John Bartlett Racing.

Once again the pole was claimed by Will Hoy in the Argo to such effect that his time was little short of the times set by the slowest of the C1 Porsches. Much hard work and burning of midnight oil had been repaid as the rebuilt car gained its second pole in a row, Will whirling the car round in a time of 1 minute 39.61 seconds. Next up came Velez/Spice, followed two

A.D.A. Engineering had mixed fortunes in the opening two rounds in Spain. The first race at Jarama brought an encouraging fourth position despite gear selection problems. In the second race at Jerez, Ian Harrower spun the car and hit the concrete wall when lying 11th overall and fourth in class. It was enough to eliminate their entry for Le Mans. 2. The old URD was making another appearance at Silverstone where it picked up points with its distant seventh place. It was another car that was not to go to the Sarthe. 3. Charles Ivey's 956-engined Tiga which ran better than ever at Silverstone thus raising hopes for Le Mans. 4. Another Tiga, this one with a Rover engine entered by Dune Motorsport. Overleaf: In the races leading up to Le Mans the car to beat in the C2 class was Spice Engineering's Spice Pontiac DFL.

seconds later by the Mallock/Leslie Ecosse. Thyrring settled into fourth spot despite problems with a cam belt breaking. The Bardon was not so lucky: John Bartlett had to buy an engine for this one race while his own was prepared but minor problems kept the car from making the grid.

At the start the Argo in the capable hands of Hoy held sway for seven glorious laps running just in front of Velez until a pipe broke in the Argo's main intercooler. Hoy headed pit-wards and lost a great deal of time while the necessary repairs were com-pleted. From that moment the Spice held the lead from Mallock in the Ecosse who was just about holding his own ahead of Thyrring in the Tiga BDT-E and Gellini in the Kelmar Racing Tiga. Gellini exited the scene when he dumped the car in the gravel at the last turn before co-drivers Ran-daccio and Venenata had even had a chance of driving, the car very little damaged but stuck fast. After about an hour's racing the Spice held a very respectable lead over the rest now headed by Thyrring's Tiga, but pit stops were looming. All 3 of the leaders dived for the pits before the 1½ hour mark was up, but the Spice proved reluctant to start before finally it roared away after dropping behind the Ecosse. Lindstrom in the Tiga proved unable to live with the pace of the leaders and dropped slowly from

them. From then on the story of the race was Spice versus Ecosse, the Scottish car taking the lead on pit stops when the Spice was reluctant to start. The Spice, though, retook the lead it was never to lose when the Ecosse began suffering from the same brake troubles it had in Jarama.

Troubles had afflicted most of the rest of the field in one way or another, worst affected being the Lucky Strike Argo which ventilated its engine in a very big way, and Ian Harrower in the ADA Gebhardt who stuffed it comprehensively, only his second acci-dent in 20 years of racing. The Tiga BDT-E retired with a broken gearbox, the URD with a broken shock absor-ber after a strong showing, the ALD on lap 31 with electrical problems, and Techno Racing's Alba with starter problems after an incident involving the Cheever Jaguar. After much argu-ment the Cosmik RBR Tiga was awarded a finish and third in class in a run involving throttle cable trouble, a misfire and suspension breakage. It was 55 laps adrift!

In the wake of this race Spice stood at the top of the C2 table, 10 points in hand over the Ecosse and even held fifth place in the overall champion-ship.

Monza two weeks later saw the British teams once again to the fore, even though the entry list was the longest so far this year with two new

entries and a welcome re-appearance. Hugh Chamberlain brought along the first of the new cars, a Spice with a Hart Turbo engine, and Dune Motor-sport their Rover-engined Tiga GC287. Putting in its first appearance of the season was the Carma Alba AR6 with drivers Martino Finotto/ Ruggera Melgrati and Pietro Silva.

Will Hoy made his hat trick with three pole positions in a row, this one in a time of 1 min. 42.62 seconds just under 2½ seconds in front of the second placed Carma Alba. The two Spices filled third and fourth positions on the grid, Velez ahead of Nick Adams in the Chamberlain car, pleased as punch with its performance. Following these came the Techno Alba, the Kelmar Tiga and, of all things, the ALD driven by Tremblay ahead of the Ecosse! The URD quali-fied next up ahead of the quartet of Tigas, all of which had some sort of problem in practice. The worse affected was the Rover-engined car which had a variety of niggly troubles conspiring to place it firmly last on the grid in a race it was destined not to start.

With pole sitter Hoy starting from the back of the grid after a push start, the Velez Spice, Finotto Alba and the charging Mallock Ecosse jumped into an immediate lead. Adams in the Chamberlain car closed up, and passed the Ecosse and Alba in quick succes-

sion while Hoy threaded his way through the pack to reach fifth place before wastegate problems cost him several laps.

The Spice duo became a single on the 33rd lap when the turbo in Adams' car let go quite spectacularly. Also out by this time was the Thyrring Tiga and the ALD.

First to pit was the Alba but the order after all had stopped still remained the same – the Spice followed by the Alba and the Ecosse. The Italian car inherited the lead when Spice himself had a frightening puncture and was forced to pit for a new tyre. When he resumed the Alba had pulled out a lead of over a minute and was a lap ahead of the Ecosse. All was not well, though, with the leader and boost control troubles caused its retirement on lap 123, handing the lead back to the Spice followed by the Ecosse. A sudden downpour in the final laps made a stop for grooved tyres essential but wiper trouble caused the red and yellow car to drop further behind leaving Gordon and Fermin to score their third successive win. The only other cars to survive the mechanical carnage of the afternoon were the URD in third spot and Hoy and Schanche at last making it to the finish in fourth place.

Nearly a month passed until the teams assembled at Silverstone for the fourth round of the Championship. One car to forego this event was the Thyrring Tiga BDT-E being all but burnt out in a fire in private testing on Thursday.

Saddest sight of the practice sessions was Martin Schanche pouring water over the turbo of his second blown Zakspeed engine. No pole this time and an expensive non-start, suspected management system failure being the cause.

Ecosse meanwhile had provided a brand new car for the Mallock/Leslie pairing, the older car being raced as back-up by Mike Wilds and ex-Lotus Formula One driver Johnny Dumfries. Cosmik GP Motorsport, the Keith Greene/Dave Prewitt/Costas Los run team, had a new Tiga-Cosworth to play with, Los himself driving partnered by ex-Ivey Tiga Porsche driver Dudley Wood, the pretty little car

going very well in practice. Dune Motorsport's Tiga-Rover was going much better than at Monza and was now looking and sounding the part. Crang and Bain recruited Swiss rally champion Jean Krucker onto the driving force with a view to Le Mans.

Sitting in the pit lane in smart black livery was the new Audi-powered ALD looking much more the business than its older BMW-engined sister, but usual new car problems meant it failed to make the grid. Two more Tigas were also present, the ex-RBR car of Ceesports Racing, soon to be Volvo powered, but with a Ford turbo installed for this race, and the Tiga GC83/4/5/6, which had a remarkable history, for the French team of Bruno Sotty/Patrick Oudet/Jean-Claude Justice.

Without the Argo the pole sitting car just had to be one of the Spices. Gordon claimed it with Nick Adams, on this occasion partnered by Graham Duxbury, second. Next up was the Cosmik Tiga, James Weaver having a quick run to help sort the new machine. The Kelmar Tiga sat on fourth spot ahead of the two Ecosse cars, the new machine slightly quicker than the old one as was to be expected. The Tiga Porsche followed, the vastly experienced pairing of Ian Taylor and Pete Lovett aboard, with the URD, in trouble with fuel feed problems, claiming eighth ahead of the Tiga Rover in ninth. Val Musetti and John Bartlett, giving himself a run in the Goodmans Bardon, qualified tenth ahead of the various Tigas and the ALD which made up the rest of the grid. The RBR car was handled for this event by Dave Andrews, Rob Peters and Max Cohen Olivar.

When the lights turned to green, Adams simply flew into the lead from Spice with both Ecosse cars next up in formation. The battle was enlivened by the presence of Weaver in the IMSA/GTP March Porsche and the URD burbling along in a not too distant fifth. Drama was visited on Gordon when on lap 13 he suffered a puncture damaging the rear bodywork, the stage thus being set for a great race on Silverstone's wide open spaces.

Adams held the lead comfortably

ahead of the Ecosse pair, Wilds exchanging ends in a hairy spin at Becketts with nothing but his pride suffering. The URD was tucked handily in fourth place. First retirement in C2 was the RBR Tiga, clutch problems putting it out on lap 42. Pit stops left the Ecosse team in first and second position until they too pitted leaving Gordie in the lead but he had an out of sync. stop to come. On lap 60 he pitted with Fermin resuming in fourth ahead of the URD but behind Leslie, Dumfries and Duxbury.

Leslie had pulled out half a lap lead as Fermin started to charge reeling in the Chamberlain car which was about to make its second stop of the afternoon. The Ecosse team held sway at the front of the field at least until their stops when Fermin grabbed the lead before handing over to Gordon 10 laps later. When the race settled down after the necessary replenishments, Gordon was through into second ahead of the Wilds/Dumfries car but about a minute behind the Mallock/Leslie car. In the Chamberlain pit there was blood all over the place, Adams having had an argument with a Silverstone hare to the considerable detriment of the beastie concerned and nose and radiator damage to the car. With the damage rectified the car resumed until Alan Berg in the Kremer Porsche shoved it rudely into the barriers at Maggots, mangling the car severely and sidelining the Porsche with rear suspension damage.

At the front the Spice car got lucky when Sigala in the Brun Porsche was punted off the track by Nielsen in the Le Mans Jaguar causing the first of the pace car periods while the Porsche was retrieved, the 60 seconds gap from the Ecosse to the Spice shrinking to nothing. When racing resumed Gordon laid one on the Ecosse, grabbing the lead at the complex on lap 142. Ray Mallock was not having any of that and promptly took it back again at the Copse. The last pit stops were taken and the Spice resumed in the lead. Dumfries in the third place Ecosse soon unlapped himself and moved away from the Spice. Leslie in the other Ecosse moved in for the kill on lap 162, passed on the straight and pulled away by 20 seconds. He nearly

1. This is the car that began as the works C1 Tiga-Chevrolet in 1983, became the first Spice-Tiga the following year with class wins in four races, was then taken over by Tim Lee-Davey who campaigned it again in the World Endurance Championship plus some Thundersports events in 1985 and then installed a DFL turbo into it to make it eligible for C1 in 1986. For 1987, it was back into the C2 Cosworth specification and driven by Bruno Sotty and Patrick Oudet. Unfortunately it was virtually destroyed in an accident at Silverstone. 2. The brand new Tiga-Cosworth of Cosmik GP Motorsport, the team formed by Keith Greene, Dave Prewitt and Costas Los.

became involved in the comprehensive shunt between the French Tiga and the Sigala/Larrauri Brun Porsche which effectively wrote both cars off, and needed the services of the pace car once more, but escaped unscathed. All that was left after that episode was a fairly simple run to the chequered flag and the first win of the year to the Scots. Into third came the second Ecosse following the Spice home and ahead of the fuel-troubled Kelmar Tiga. The Ivey Tiga-Porsche made it to the flag in fifth place with the

Tiga-Rover next followed by the URD. Last across the line was the ALD ahead of two non-classified cars, the Metaxa Tiga and the Sheldon Ceesports Tiga. The only other retirement of the afternoon was the Bardon which demolished its engine in a big way.

As a pointer to Le Mans itself the test day took place on the 17th May with the Spice setting the pace with a time of 3m 45.46s, ahead of Nick Adams and Richard Jones who recorded a time of 3m 47s in the

Chamberlain Spice, followed by the Ecosse on 3m 53s set by David Leslie. Dune Motorsport brought along their Tiga-Rover and in Crang's hands it recorded a time of 4m 02.09s. Both ALD cars were off the pace, the BMW-engined car recording a time of 4m 15.11s, some 10 seconds ahead of the Audi-engined car.

The Spice cars certainly looked favourites to win C2 but Le Mans plays by its own rules, anything could happen and usually does: 24 hours is a long time.

DEREK BELL and AUTOGLASS

Autoglass have supported Derek Bell over the past three seasons and enjoyed with him his successes at Le Mans and his two World Sportscar Championship titles.

Derek Bell's sportscar career opened when John Wyer invited him to join the Gulf-Porsche 917 team in 1971, partnering the legendary Jo Siffert, and since then Bell has won 35 International Championship races. In the 63 year history of the French classic Le Mans race, only Jacky Ickx, his former driving partner, has won the race more times than Bell, with six victories to Bell's five.

Bell and his USA co-driver, Al Holbert, made history by winning four 24 hour races in succession: the 1986 and 1987 Daytona 24 Hour Race and the 1986 and 1987 Le Mans.

At Le Mans not only did Autoglass support Derek Bell, but all the works Porsches, as they did at Silverstone, Monza, Jarama, Jerez and Brands Hatch.

Indeed Bell has Autoglass and Shell Oils to thank for their financial support in sponsoring the Joest Porsche 962 in the Shell Oils 1000 kms race at Brands Hatch in 1986, for his second World title.

LEFT: Derek's long standing partner in the factory Porsche team is Hans Stuck seen here powering the Porsche on its way to victory at Le Mans. RIGHT: World Champion though he is, Derek is one of the most genial personalities in motor sport.

POSTE HASTE

Flash! Bang! Wallop! The launching of Swiftair Ecosse in the satanic majesty of London's trendy Hippodrome nightspot, all matt black'n'mirrors, was a noisy and illuminating affair, the arrival of their flame red car heralding a crescendo of sound and vision, fanfares and fireworks, lights and lasers.

At Ecurie Ecosse thirty years separate today's dream from the reality of yesterday, decades united by a name and single objective: to win Le Mans. It is not only a passage of time but also space, the grace of dignified Edinburgh far removed from their present base in a Northamptonshire farmyard, any pouting and preening done not by West End trendies but chickens . . . And the 'Hype of the Hip' is a long way from bleak Silverstone one week later as Ray Mallock commenced pre-season testing, islands of ice in the pitlane a reminder of winter, hope springing eternal.

Ray was heavily involved in Viscount Downe's Nimrod when Hugh McCaig first approached him about building a Le Mans challenger, the wealthy Edinburgh businessman/ enthusiast having rekindled the flame and revived the name of Ecurie Ecosse earlier in 1983. Initially both projects would run concurrently, until the storm abated on the V8 thunder. Mallock, for his part, had finally become disillusioned with single seaters when a FOCA Formula One test promised as winner of the '81 Formula Atlantic championship failed to materialise, the advent of Group C the following year a timely alternative.

The first Ecosse was a modified de Cadenet. Second on its debut at Monza, the following results tailed off until it was finally destroyed in a horrifying shunt at Brands Hatch during the British GP supporting Thundersports race, Ray fortunate to escape medium rare after being trapped in the ensuing fire.

Its replacement, the first genuine Ecosse chassis, was penned by Graham Humphreys who has also been responsible for the Spice Fiero. His brief was to concentrate on favourable Le Mans characteristics like low drag and a small frontal area rather than more generalised criteria, hence the small wheels and brakes. Unfortunately the Sarthe did not reciprocate in generosity of spirit and despite eight C2 class wins – plus last year's Teams' title – the revived association had but one Le Mans finish to its credit from four attempts as they prepared for the 1987 classic. And all were aware that this marked the thirtieth anniversary of their illustrious predecessors' wonderful one – two . . .

RIGHT: 1987 was important to the Ecosse team as it marked the 30th anniversary of the team's outright win at Le Mans. After winning the 1986 World Championship, team owner Hugh McCaig very much wanted history to repeat itself at the Sarthe circuit.

Trust Swiftair to get there fast!

Attach importance to your overseas letters. For just a small fee plus postage you can use Swiftair, Royal Mail's worldwide express letter service.

Swiftair letters receive priority treatment — not just in this country but in over 120 countries abroad. This helps them to get there up to 24 hours faster than normal. That way they'll know you mean business.

Swiftair is available at all post offices. To find out more about how Swiftair can express your company's overseas mail, dial 100 and ask for Freefone Swiftair.

They'll know you mean business. Swiftair

Royal
Mail

At the spectacular launch of the Swiftair sponsorship in March 1987 Cedric Briscoe, the General Manager of the Royal Mail's International Letters division, said: "This is a hard-nosed commercial venture. We wanted to raise the profile of Swiftair, our express airmail service, and link it with speed, reliability and success. What better way to do this than with World Champions Ecurie Ecosse?"

Marvellous results so far this season have shown that Ecurie Ecosse and Swiftair are going places together.

Huw Evans, the Swiftair Marketing Manager, underlined the value of the sponsorship. "It works on three levels. In the wider advertising and promotion context, large numbers of people see Swiftair on the track and in the main media. Ours is probably the most photogenic car on the circuit, thanks to our promotions agency CSS, and the Swiftair name is highly visible.

"In the narrower field of customer hospitality it is an out-and-out winner. The effect of a trip to the races, wearing Swiftair colours, is incredible: before the race the drivers come and meet our guests so that when they are trackside the customers know about the race, the circuit and their team – and they quickly become part of that team.

"Thirdly, the Swiftair Ecosse and the team have proved a brilliant partnership within the Post Office. Our staff newspaper *Courier* has consistently featured the team in its articles. As a result of those efforts we will have over 1,000 staff in a special grandstand at Brands Hatch on July 26 for the 1,000 Kilometres race – another highlight in an exciting first season."

They hit town on Monday after an overnight ferry crossing from Portsmouth to Le Havre, drivers and key personnel soon ensconced in a rented private chateau, others billeted elsewhere. At the circuit, in 'Le Village' Ecosse pitched high upon the slope, their brightly coloured transporters easily biggest in class, attendant vehicles gathered around much like a wagon train preparing against an injun attack. When it came on Wednesday evening it looked as if the Red Man was about to lose out to the Blackfoot . . .

After encouraging trial results, including the Le Mans Test Day a week after that morale boosting class one – three at just-down-the-roade Silverstone, a decision had been made to use Yokohama tyres in lieu of their normal Avons, Melksham rubber only retained for wet purposes. Three deflations during the first two hour session almost scalped that master plan, these problems soon traced to the seal of rubber on rim, air being allowed to return whence it came in a most alarming manner. Fortunately assistance was readily available to resolve this crisis, no shortage of willing helpers and experts including Max Bostrom, the man from Dymag Wheels also a member of Ecosse's own think tank. No need to send for the cavalry – it was already there!

So were the gearbox gremlins getting set to manifest themselves all weekend. Mallock parked '102' along Mulsanne just before 8 o'clock when a spigot retaining reverse idler gear sheared off: "There was a clunking noise and then it sounded like something dragging along the ground.

David Leslie celebrates the Ecosse's class win at the Autoglass 1000km at Silverstone.

Actually it was the gear machining its way through the side casing . . ."

It took some two hours repairing '102' to good health, getting out again only during the rain as it fell during the last thirty minutes of Wednesday's late session, long enough only for Ray and David Leslie to complete their mandatory night driving requirements, Marc Duez having to await the morrow. Meanwhile, unhindered by those transmission traumas, Messrs Wilds, Delano and Petery had completed their qualifying procedures aboard '101', a snippet of good news on a bad day.

These dramas had upset the normal well drilled routine d'Eccosias, their careful game plan having scored about as many points as a Turkish entry in the Eurovision Song Contest, pushed aside by virtually losing a whole day for their newer car, there being still much to do.

These dramas had an effect of dampening spirits if only temporarily, though not enough to dilute their determination, the dry if somewhat clouded humour of clan chief McCaig still evident as Thursday's afternoon rainstorm flooded the paddock: "The only certainty is that we will start the race. This is not our darkest hour: here they are all dark – even in daylight!"

Fortunately the outlook was brighter, the storm acting as if a cleansing agent, their ensuing qualifying sessions passing without incident save for a clash of more than temperaments between Mallock and a Toyota at the Ford Chicane, '102' losing a rear wing end plate but otherwise undamaged. Now the quickest Ecosse, it would line up on Row 17, immediately ahead of '101', Mallock and Mike Wilds destined to undertake those first vital stints.

As they waited on the grid, those final few moments before setting off behind the Mercedes pace car, both drivers went through the ritual of last minute checks; trusting nothing had been overlooked, believing in faith, hope and an untroubled fast run. At that moment neither they nor anybody else probably had time or inclination to think back to a winter's day in ol' London town when the partnership between Swiftair and Ecurie Ecosse was announced, their stated aim being victory at Le Mans. But everyone hoped what had virtually started with a bang would not end in a whimper.

When David Hobbs first raced at Le Mans, Ferrari were the dominant force at the Sarthe, Phil Hill/Oliver Gendebien's 330LM leading home a pair of GTOs from an entry filled with such diversities as Rene Bonnets and an Aston Martin P212. A muted challenge from Jaguar relied on Lightweight E types from Briggs Cunningham and friends, the Porsche threat still to be voiced. Our conversation started by transporting him back from today's 962C to a Lotus Elite. It was 1962.

"The race was low key compared to now, only my second or third overseas event," says the man whose motorsport career had started three years earlier by driving, of all things, a Morris Oxford automatic!: "My main memory is of a very successful debut, winning the 1300cc GT class and Thermal Index of Efficiency, eighth overall with Frank Gardner. It was the old circuit, the old White House; I remember the cutting up to there as being a particularly exciting part of the track but realise it would be impractical in this day and age. I remember the long Sunday to the finish, it was very hot, the starter in the road flagging us in . . . Other than that my memories are scant, it was so long ago."

Indeed his main recollections are not of on-track action but off-track dramas, continuing:

"When we came here, scrutineering used to be in a field at the back and the track's technical engineer was the local baker or some such local dignitary. Part of the deal was a Lotus 23 driven by Jim Clark and Trevor Taylor but they turned it down, going through all sorts of machinations until finally giving us a reason that as the front wheels had four studs and the rears six therefore the fronts must be unsafe! Mike Costin (now Cosworth) and Colin Chapman fought this very forcibly, explaining the fronts do not have any strain of driving the car, while having new wheels flown out from England. That stopped them for a few minutes then they said the car did not comply to the spirit of the regulations and was withdrawn. The whole reason for all this was those Panhards which always won the Indexes, but is was highly unlikely the Lotus 23 would have finished. We went and won anyway, so they need not have gone through all

that bullshit! It was a satisfying win from Lotus and England's point of view, to take those prizes the French coveted so much. They are a funny bunch, very French – apart from that they're fine!"

David has now participated in eighteen Sarthois classics, his experience in this and an enormous variety of other mediums the equal to anyone. Third here in both 1969 and '84 plus fourth twice in recent years, victory has, as yet, been denied, but he is adamant he knows what it takes to win:

"Luck. There is absolutely no way of calling form on this race, it is like the Grand National. For Jacky Ickx to have won it six times is u-n-b-e-l-i-e-v-a-b-l-e, absolutely. I just do not know how anybody can be *that* lucky, *that* blessed. It's uncanny. And Derek (Bell) too . . . Every time they win people say 'Well they are so good, so easy on the equipment, so this, so the other . . . It just drives me *crazy*! The sort of things that have put me out of contention have had nothing to do with *my* driving. In 1968 Paul Hawkins and I could easily have won it, we were faster than Rodriguez and Bianchi, but our engine went. We had voiced doubts about it in practice so they had a look to find the exhaust pipe touching the frame, saying that is what we can 'feel' . . . The next year, when Ickx won after that incredible dice with Hermann, a brake pipe was cut by a wheel weight the Firestone guys put on in the wrong place. Mike Hailwood and I finished the race in third place, nothing else going wrong. If that had not happened . . . In 1970, again with Mike, he hit a car which had crashed around the Dunlop Curve. It happened early on but we and Attwood/Hermann had 4.5 litre engines with almost everybody else using 5.0 litres. All the fives blew up and Richard went on to win. When Mike crashed we were ahead of them . . ."

It was certainly an eventful era for Hobbs: 1971, partnering Mark Donohue in the fabulous Sunoco 512LM their engine blew for the only time all year. Twelve months later a certain third place in the Matra steamroller was lost when the gearbox broke an hour from home. He continues:

"I categorically should have won in 1984 when driving with Sarel (van der

Merwe) and Strieff, having a one lap lead after fourteen hours when it went on to five cylinders. The reason is almost certainly a bit of rag left in the plenum chamber on the warm up lap which probably set the rot in on burning a valve out. There had been an engine change, I went out of the pits, the throttle stuck but I had to do a whole lap. Everything seemed to be okay but the damage had probably already been done. We still came third . . . In fact, in '83, the fuel metering unit broke a shaft. There is no strain, no load, you cannot hurt it. Everyone just stood around saying 'Blow me. I've never seen that happen before'. We were third or fourth when it happened and might have won or been close . . ."

All of these memories are recalled without jealousy, bitterness or rancour, only a genuine racer's disappointment at not fully in control of his own destiny:

"Those are the sort of things which can happen all the time. We could be leading the race by ten laps when I put it into a fence. It would be the first time in two or three years but it could happen. Miss a shift, flat spot the tyres, have to make an extra stop . . . There is a tremendous latitude for making a complete balls up here. With three drivers, eight hours each at 130mph average speed there are plenty of places to make a right cock up! No one is invincible, there is not a driver here who hasn't made a mistake. Sometimes you are a bit lucky as to where and when you make it. If you have a flat tyre there you've had it, if you have it here you are laughing. There is no way of telling. It is an absolute lottery . . ."

With more racing behind him than ahead, what does the future hold for David Hobbs?

"I had my brother with me here twenty five years ago and he is here today. My son Greg was only one month old then, now he is racing himself. If I have an ambition left in racing it is to do Le Mans with him in a good car, but he needs more experience yet before he is ready for this place."

Sadly, experience sometimes counts for nothing at Le Mans, our conversation lasting for longer than the Joest Porsche would do come Saturday.

LES FANS DU MANS

To quote a famous saying, the Le Mans 24 hour race is a race for the British held in France and this year that statement seemed more relevant than ever as upwards of 40,000 British made the journey to Le Mans. From Beauties to Boozers, Brokers to Brickies they made their way to the home of British motor racing in France.

Why, we wanted to know, did they do so. We asked the questions and some of the answers gave an insight into the lunacy that is Le Mans.

First people we spoke to, albeit very briefly, were Christopher & Sue Bloy who must win the prize for bravery/persistence and a special kind of eccentricity having driven all the way from their home in Leicester in a 1933 Austin 7 with top speed around 42 mph, the little car apparently going splendidly with no hiccups en route. Regulars at Le Mans they try to bring a different and unusual machine each year, and would be back next year in some other exotica.

Friday lunchtime, and the last great watering hole of the British Raj, the bar des 24 heures at Hunaudieres. Now we hoped to get down to the nitty-gritty and find the real reasons for the annual pilgrimage to Le Mans, and after one or two drinks we found that our questions were answered more easily, as the bar and surrounding area were stacked to the gills with British registered cars and their occupants.

What's this, a German registered Suzuki jeep with Union Jacks flying and the music from 633 squadron playing loud and clear on its cassette player. All was to be revealed when we talked to the driver, Steve Thompson. Originally from Birmingham, Steve now works in the body styling department of Audi in Ingolstadt and had taken 18 hours to drive down. Decked out in a pilot's suit, which was complete with a strategic bottle opener and RAF Jaguar squadron badges hanging off it, it was Steve's 6th year at the event and he had met some 14 of his mates from round the Coventry area. Some of those mates were with him, Pete Ingram, Phil Gauld, Paul Beech and George Bradshaw having left home at 6.30 pm on Wednesday evening. They arrived via Portsmouth–Le Havre and were there to support the Jags, Steve being there for "The Occasion". The lads were obviously out to have a good time and complaints about the price of the beer were the only thing that would spoil their weekend, though they had taken 5 crates with them in case they got thirsty back at the camp site.

For a bit of glamour and sparkle, we asked the lovely and shapely Jennifer Grinley, down for the first time with her boyfriend Mark Backup and his brother Simon, her thoughts. Jenny from Chester and the two lads from Manchester had made their way through Paris straight to Les Hunaudieres in Simon's RS Turbo Escort. They were there to support Richard Jones and would still have turned up even if the Jags had not been there. Jenny was very eloquent when expressing her anticipation of the race, but was absolutely appalled at the price of the beer and the motorway tolls. What she reserved most of her ire for, however, was the state of the toilets comparing them unfavourably to the Elephant house at Chester Zoo. One good suggestion Jenny came up with was the idea of a survival guide for first timers at Le Mans, a very bright idea we thought.

For some people the cars are the all important factor in the race, one such is Michael Pullen from Chichester who had possibly the easiest journey of all to the race. Mike owns a total of 17 cars dating from a 1902 Hanzer to the E-type he was using for the race, though all but the E-type are pre-1939 and include 3 × 1935 Morrises, a '34 Rover, a '33 Ford and a '35 Bentley Park Ward. Arriving in time for the Thursday practice Mike has done Le Mans for the past 4 years, and is now completely hooked. He really could not care less who would win the race but would have liked the Jaguars to win if possible. As with all the people we spoke to Mike says that it is the atmosphere that grabs him – the build up to the race for him is something quite unique.

The Poseurs du Mans award this year goes to a certain part of what was most certainly a section of the BMW Club of Great Britain with their personalised number plates, in-car telephones, and over-loud talk.

So there you have it. What makes people suffer it, I don't know. It can be cold, wet, too hot or any combination of all that. It is invariably filthy, smelly and unhygienic, it is tiring, mind-blowing and energy-sapping. What is it about Le Mans, I don't know? See you same time, same place next year.

THE CAT.

THE CREAM.

"Congratulations from Castrol on a successful year."

Castrol (UK) Ltd., Burmah House, Pipers Way, Swindon, Wiltshire SN3 1RE.

BRUN MOTORSPORT

JOEST RACING

KREMER

BLR LIQUI MOLY

PRIMAGAZ

PORSCHE AG

TWR SILK CUT

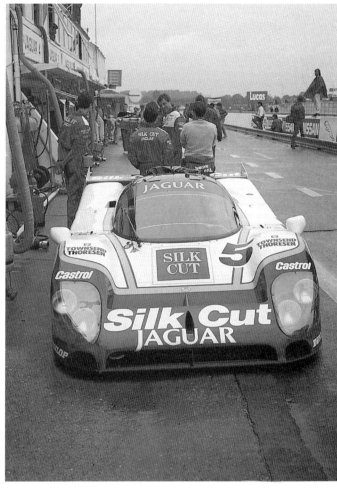

PRIMAGAZ

NISMO

ITALYA SPORTS

NISMO

TOYOTA TEAM TOMS

GRAFF RACING

DEL BELLO RACING

SECATEVA

KOUROS RACING

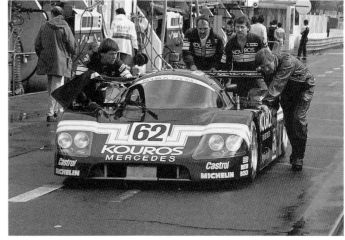

SWIFTAIR ECOSSE

BARTLETT RACING

ROLAND BASSALER

SPICE ENGINEERING

JOSÉ THIBAULT

TIGA TEAM FORD DENMARK

LUIGA TAVERNA – TECHNORAGING

LUCKY STRIKE – SCHANCHE

OLINDO JACOBELLI

COSMIK RACING WITH GP MOTORSPORT

VETIR RACING TEAM

CHARLES IVEY RACING

CHAMBERLAIN ENGINEERING

CEESPORTS RACING

AUTOMOBILES LOUIS DESCARTES

DUNE MOTORSPORT

ROY BAKER RACING

DAHM CARS RACING TEAM

MAZDASPEED

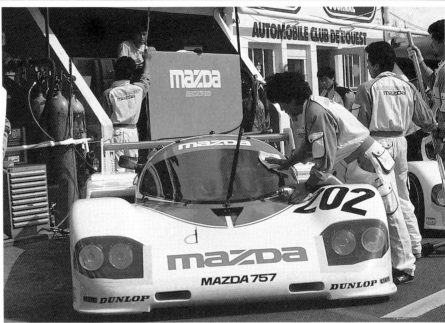

PORSCHE AG

NICK'S KNACK

Nick Adams has been racing since 1974, winning a variety of Clubmans' titles before moving into Sports 2000, Formula Atlantic and finally finding his niche in Thundersports/Sports Prototypes. Since his post in Swiftair Ecosse became misdirected, Nick has sought solace in Hugh Chamberlain's Spice Hart turbocar, the man proving quick, the machine so far unable to go the distance without dramas.

During the relative peace of Friday lunchtime – overlooked by an inflatable doll aback the team's transporter! – I asked him to describe the lap which brought his C2 pole position:

"We ran on 1.4 bar boost which adds about 150 bhp, giving probably about 600 bhp in total, which is quite good for a C2 car.

"Past the pits, fourth into fifth, I did not get the new corner right. Normally I go in too slow, this time too fast. It's one of those corners where you think 'Get it right Adams. You can go a lot quicker than this' but this time I went in so fast I nearly did not make it, scrabbled through . . . Down the hill, take the Esses in third, snatch fourth along to Tertre Rouge, down to third for the corner . . . Onto the straight, I saw over 8000 rpm by the Restaurant des 24 Heures, I knew it was going to be a quick lap. When I got to the trees just before the Kink it was still wet, not just damp, wet-wet. I figured I was going so fast it probably would stick to the ground as I went through and it did. At the end of the straight I was pulling 8800 rpm, we were very chuffed with that . . . Second gear around Mulsanne Corner, I overtook the BLR Porsche on the run down to 'Indy', it was cruising, through the box, it was still a bit damp there, but not really a problem . . . Indianapolis, the first one in fourth and the next in third: Arnage in second . . . Up to the Porsche Curves, fourth through there, then onto the Ford Chicanes, third for the first, second for the second.

"The nearest I came to spinning it was there, in full sight of everybody in the pitlane. Completely sideways, I went up onto the rumble strips on the outside, thought 'what a pillock I'll look if I spin it here'. I didn't and that was that.

"I actually came in to have A11s put on as I did not think my time would be quick enough. It would have been a lot quicker if I hadn't mucked it up, a good two seconds quicker. It was a very satisfying result. I did not get to bed until four o'clock this morning, went up to the bar and consumed an ale or two."

Or was it one – point – four? Cheers, Nick!

As results of the General Election became known, thousands of Britons headed for the Channel ports and a hasty exit.

Whether their political hues were of blue or red or yellow mattered not, the cries now for purple, support of Jaguar evident everywhere as ancient caravanettes and modern coaches, 'rep' Sierras and replica C-types filled ferries then highways: all roads leading to Le Mans.

They found many there before them, the hardiest souls having arrived in time for scrutineering and signing-on, 'Vérifications' commencing on Tuesday within the shadow of this city's mighty Gothic cathedral, the ramparts and flying buttresses testimony to more than an unholy trinity of speed, fuel economy and reliability. Drivers crowded around to complete their own personal particulars, cars waited to be funnelled through their checks, the ritual to take about ninety minutes, longer than many would last come Saturday afternoon. Two Brun 962Cs and NDB's private Sauber arrived aboard a 'Toleman' delivery transporter, the Kouros examples in box trailers, the strange Thibault Chevron as if beamed down from some alien planet. Despite being midway on the official list, first through were T.W.R., a pattern they hoped to maintain all week.

Realistically they and everyone else knew pole position was beyond the scope of a normally aspirated engine, seven litres of V-12 or not, a fuel enrichment device no match for a turbo boost knob, their best hope being Row Two.

No problem; that was the response to any enquiries about practice maladies, all three Coventry cats having a remarkably trouble-free couple of days, Wednesday's sessions confined to race tests as the three Silverstone pairings were supplemented by Armin Hahne and Win Percy as reserve drivers, neither of whom were sure to race, Winston's cup destined to runneth over. All were brimming with confidence in their machinery, each one convinced they had what it takes to win at Le Mans: John Watson and

Raul Boesel expressing only the concerns of many regarding weather, circuit safety and speed differentials, the Brazilian suggesting they were good for keeping one's attention focused . . . Meanwhile John Neilsen warmed to the task ahead: "When I come here for first practice I don't like it but after a time you get used to the atmosphere. Now I'm looking forward to it."

So was everyone else including Roger Silman, TWR's team manager advising on Thursday lunchtime: "Yesterday we ran practice as we had wished, save for a threat of rain coming away very contented. We would like to have gone slightly quicker and may be able to do that today." They did, Eddie Cheever marginally faster than either Martin Brun-

dle or Jan Lammers, all in the three-twenty fours, their times good enough to take positions three, four and five on Saturday's grid. Row Two was secure, the objective achieved. On schedule, as planned. It was all looking good for Silk Cut Jaguar: no problem.

Unlike up the pitlane *chez* Roth-mans Porsche where Bob Wollek pipped Hans Stuck for pole position by ⁴/₁₀₀ths of a second with his lap of 3'21.09, both recording their times during Wednesday's early session, any pleasure in top slot for Strasbourg's favourite son muted by an accident which befell Price Cobb near the end of that same period.

1. The heart of the Jaguar. 2. Spares neatly lined up prior to the race.
3. The fastest XJR on the straight.
4. The highest placed Jaguar on the grid.

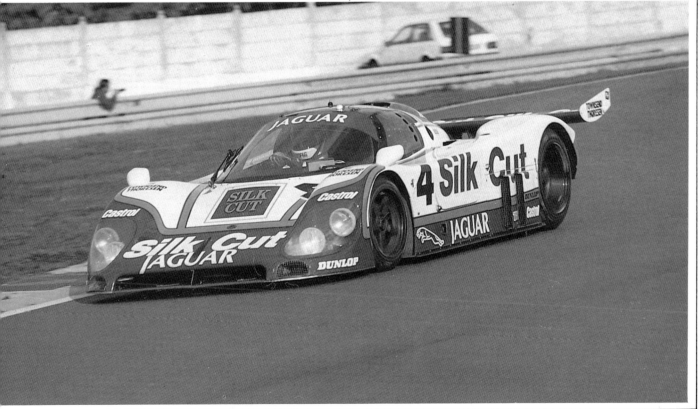

1

↓2

3

4

1. The cockpit and dashboard of one of the Jaguars. 2. The works Porsche that failed to start the race due to an accident in practice that demolished it. 3. All three Jaguars underwent thorough preparation before the race. 4. John Nielsen in practice before the race. 5. Derek Bell in the cockpit of the Porsche before setting out on a practice session.

5

In the pitlane word of such happenings travels swiftly, all soon aware a 'factory' Porsche had gone missing, fate unknown. Gradually details started to filter through: Rothmans 19 was off near Maison Blanche, safety barriers unable to arrest its progress, fire had ensued. Everyone held their breath. The wait for more information seemed interminable, in fact only seconds: car destroyed, driver unharmed. That was okay, pitlane cameraderie not extending to machinery, the storm of sound as another challenger blasted past the pits resonating loud against a low cloud base, pitching attention once again on the job in hand. Back to business, there is a race to be won.

The accident left a gap in Weissach's hopes and aspirations big enough to drive a Jag through, Herr Falk having no spare vehicle to call upon following a calamity in hot testing the previous week. Now, in the cold light of an overcast French evening, it became clear there would only be two factory prepared 962Cs braced against a three clawed attack from Jaguar, the wheel of fortune again turning in favour of Coventry, Kidlington's ray of sunshine glowing ever brighter as night descended over the Sarthe.

Rothmans redeployed their depleted forces: Vern Schuppan joining Wollek/Jochen Mass, Kees Neirop replacing Steckonnig aboard the four-wheel-drive 961, only last year's victorious trio of Derek Bell/Alvah Holbert/Stuck unchanged by events, Cobb off to pastures renewed at BLR. And it was Stuck who had the last sobering words about the demise of his erstwhile American team-mate: "They need armco posts every two metres instead of four. The posts collapsed, they just fell over. He was lucky it went in with the back, it saved his legs . . .".

If Porsche were hoping their customers would back them in the fight to fend off Jaguar then qualifying did little to promote much optimism, the final three places in the top four rows taken by Yves Courage's Cougar, albeit with a flat six powerplant, and a duet of Sauber C9s, their basso-profundo V8s particularly singing in

the rain. Indeed on a wet track all three of these Michelin shod projectiles were especially impressive, a situation prompting Herve Regout to remark laughingly: "Dunlop have not made a decent rain tyre for thirty years. I hope it rains for at least fifteen hours!" and although said in jest it epitomised the spirit and optimism emanating from the local team from Stuttgart-en-France.

Not so Kouros. Reconfirmed by the excellent showing of Johnny Dumfries on his first acquaintance with team and track, some spoke of Peter Sauber's latest creations as dark horses for overall honours but all was not well with the Hinwil machines. "We have got lots of reliability problems – engine bearings, gearbox, things which come with Le Mans . . ." stated Mike Thackwell, his voice seemingly re-

1. Yves Courage's Cougar qualified well in sixth position. 2. Quadruple Le Mans winner Henri Pescarolo beside the Sauber-Mercedes. 3. 'Come out, it's no good you 'iding in there – you've got to go and qualify.' 4. The Hinwil built machines were superbly turned out. 5. Prior to the race, the Sauber-Mercedes were considered as the dark horses for overall honours. Overleaf: Although car 62 was entered for Dumfries and Ganassi, it was also qualified by Mike Thackwell.

signed to disappointment as he listed the faults, tailing off: "We are going to try to finish . . .". Just as last year, Kouros had underwritten the event, just as last year their public relations presence was very high profile, just as last year they seemed destined to an ignominious failure. If these were dark horses they were already destined for the knacker's yard . . .

While the prospects of quadruple winner Henri Pescarolo looked unsure, former BRM FI colleague François Migault slipped ahead of him in the timesheets as second best local hero, both conceding seven seconds to impressive comingman Pierre-Henri Raphanel with the Cougar C20. Migault's time was set aboard the older WM Peugeot, good enough only for Row Seven, eight places ahead of Roger Dorchy in a P87 of which much was expected along Mulsanne following reports of 258 mph/416 kph on a public road a week earlier. Alas it could manage only 381 kph, consider-

ably faster than anyone else although well short of 'Target Quatrecents', the team adamant it reached terminal velocity *after* passing a timing beam set up in the wrong spot. As arguments continued, *La Gloire de La Belle France* at stake, the Secateva car appeared resigned to it all, hinged front and rear bodywork sections seemingly forever pointed skywards as if in surrender.

Walter Brun's press release had an air of submission about it: indicating an intention to pursue a future at IMSA, his final comment being: "The good times for private teams in Europe are over . . .". It could be right, particularly in his own case, if Le Mans form is studied; last year all three Brun Porsches qualifying in the top dozen, this time best only twelfth while two others languished in midfield. Slow to catch on was Brun 3 for Rothmans Canada's 'Crazy Canucks', livery more splendid than performance, while even further back came the car leased to GDBA for Belmondo, Trolle and de Thoisy, a less likely trio never to carry the coveted Number One. Although all Porsche privateers have been considerably overshadowed by their mentors this term, such a marked lack of competitive edge from the reigning World Teams' champions was indeed disappointing, the 'King of the Pokies' having apparently decreed to take a share of royalties rather than a good shot at the jackpot. Only their Fortuna car seemed to have any chance of real success, although unlikely to repeat its hard won second place of last year despite the continued presence of Oscar Larrauri.

Sharing the sixth row was Joest's Blaupunkt entry, two places behind its sister car bedecked in that legendary livery of Taka Q, still bearing the famous Number Seven. Their 956 may have gone, replaced by a 962 C under current regulations, but the mystique surrounding this living embodiment of Sarthe success remains strong, its very presence a threat to all and sundry. Their impressive record of recent years, the famous if undisclosed 'secret ingredient' and a very strong driver line up – including Stanley Dickens,

Chip Robinson and double winner Hurley Haywood – all boded well for the Absteinach equipe, their practice sessions a model of speed and efficiency, causing David Hobbs to remark: "You do not have to be the quickest to win here but every year I've done well we have been there or thereabouts." With Sarel van der Merwe and Frank Jelinski highly impressive during their qualifying runs nobody was likely to sidetrack Reinhold's expresses from the betting.

1. The coveted Number One was carried by Belmondo, Trolle and de Thoisy.
2. The best Brun car to qualify was car Number Two which still only managed 12th. 3. The Rothman's Canada livery was more splendid than its performance in practice. 4. The Taka Q car still bore the famous Number Seven with which Joest won the 1984 and 1985 races.
5. The presence of this car at Le Mans was a very real threat to both the works Porsche and Jaguar teams. 6. It was the best private Porsche to qualify.
Overleaf: Joest's Blaupunkt entry qualified two places behind its sister car in 11th place.

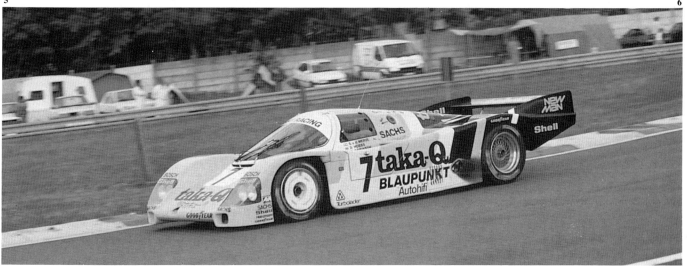

More good money was going on the unique Britten Lloyd Racing 962 GTi, Liqui Moly's familiar colour scheme replaced by the bright red of Takefuji, a Japanese finance house. Also replaced was their special qualifying engine, Jonathon Palmer gliding pitwards at 18H27 on Wednesday to report: "A piston went halfway down Mulsanne before we had even completed a full lap!" and a frantic unit change was underway, BLR installing the replacement, their race engine, in little over two hours ready for the night session, their Le Mans challenge delayed but undaunted. Once restored to good health, Britain's 'other' C1 team never missed a beat, Doctor Palmer making excellent progress aided by James Weaver and Price Cobb, the American recuperating from his Rothmans contretemps with those for whom he competed last year, Pierre Petit unable to make the initial cut.

Three more Porsches helped fill the grid, two from a Kremer team still shocked by the loss of Jo Gartner and an Obermaier example for Primagaz, all firmly ensconced in midfield with five Japanese warriors, the Nissans and Toyotas yet to make Eastern promise into Ouestern reality. Nismo went about matters in a more circumspect manner than twelve months previous, only Olofsson's private car bringing them much attention with a chassis damaging off on Wednesday, while at Team Tom's all John Wickham could complain about was slight fuel feed problems and lack of straightline speed, their two litre

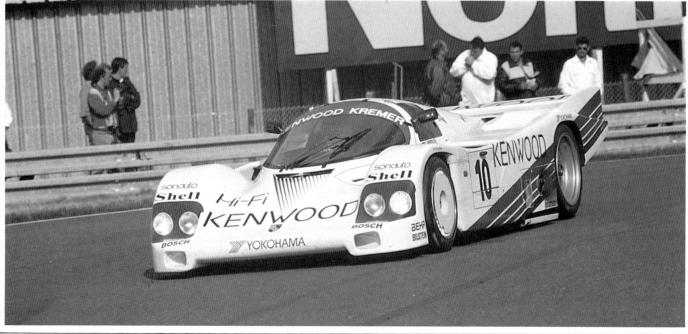

turbocharged straight fours giving away too much on Mulsanne. And 'away' was the four letter word most in the thoughts of Chairman Jones, the former World Champion not disguising his pleasure at just being there, the closest thing to his heart surely a Qantas timetable . . .

Japan's third representation came with a pair of Mazdas heading not only the Del Bello Sauber and Graff Rondeau as final C1 contenders but, more importantly, the Rothmans 961 which represented their only threat for

IMSA honours. They had forgone their traditional Silverstone 'loosener' with Nigel Stroud's remodelled chassis while the same six pilots were employed as last year, the result hopefully to be better as neither lasted until dawn, their shrill triple rotary engines sure to keep awake the demons of darkness. Sharing Row Fourteen, Mazdaspeed would be two rungs up on René Metge and Gaston Rahier, no doubt their thoughts often straying to far off places, the Tenere Desert, the road to Dakar . . .

1. The Britten Lloyd Racing 962 GTi in its unfamiliar Takefuji livery qualified well in 10th place. 2. The Nissen/Weidler/Takahashi Kremer car was just a makeweight in qualifying. 3. The other Kremer car did a far better job in practice. 4. Toyota Number 37 qualified in 16th place, two places behind its sister. 5. The Obermaier Porsche had a careful practice to qualify 18th. 6. The Nissan R87E could only qualify in 20th place.

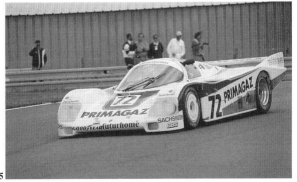

1. The two Mazda 757s, in the IMSA class, qualified on the 14th row, Number 202 one place behind its sister car.
2. The Nissan team were disappointed to qualify the R87E on only 17th spot.
3. The Italya Nissan R86V qualified in a lowly 24th place. 4. The Jones/Lees/Elgh Toyota qualified 14th. 5. The Porsche 961, the only other car in the IMSA class, qualified behind both Mazdas.

1

2

3

4

Closer to home came a fight for C2 grid honours, Gordon Spice taking overnight class pole only to see Nick Adams beat him by a full two seconds, the 3'40.02 bettering five 'big bangers' including a pair of Brunmobiles, keeping it all in the family as they lined up 22nd and 25th overall. Fermin Velez and Phillipe de Henning shared Gordy's yellow peril, its Dianetique livery showing well under sombre skies, the only cloud on their horizon being when the Spaniard slid off on that same oil slick which caught out Price Cobb thus damaging the Fiero's rear bodywork. Hugh Chamberlain's men would probably have settled for that indiscretion despite the fillip of being top of their form, the Spice Hart having all manner of difficulties notably regarding waterworks.

Another to suffer in qualifying was Ecurie Ecosse, the spotlight truly on their bright Swiftair coachwork, everyone well aware of *that* anniversary. Day one was a disaster for McCaig's Marvels, a spate of tyre deflations then a broken gearbox upsetting their normal circumspect qualifying routine, Thursday much improved. Fourth and sixth in class, they would form up in line astern on Saturday.

Completing the top half dozen were a pair of Tigas, Howden Ganley's company being second largest manufacturer there with seven entries of which six would start. Heading this in-house battle came Charles Ivey's Porsche turbo GC287 with Tom Dodd Noble doing the business in qualifying and hoping for a class win as per last year, while Patrick Oudet/Vetir looked for a happier ending than at Silverstone, the DFL powered device totally rebuilt following that horrific shunt. The four remaining Tigas all formed a block a few rows further back, the variations on a theme shown by Dune's Metro V6, Cosworth V8s for RBR and Cosmik/GP plus Thorkild Thyrring using a BDT turbo. Amongst the pilots of this intrepid band there featured many an experienced name: John Cooper, Bruno Sotty, Aussie Crang and Moroccan Cohen-Olivar – men from differing backgrounds with the same goal in mind, David Andrews, Dudley Wood

and John Sheldon while Ian Harrower climbed aboard the Danish entry when his own ADA failed to materialise.

Also seeking an alternative was Tim Lee Davey, searching the paddock on Tuesday, his presence much in evidence, his C1 Tiga turbocar nowhere to be found. What he discovered was the Goodmans Bardon thus joining M. Boutinaud and Mr Donovan to share the penultimate row with Roland Bassaler's Sauber C6, its beautiful colour scheme of last year now replaced by yeucky yellow which appeared to have been applied with a yardbroom . . .

A few metres further behind came Richard Piper's ex-Michael Andretti Royale RP40. Entered by American dragster ace Olindo Jacobelli it overcame a variety of problems, mainly electrical, to head that weird Chevron for whom only owner Thibault actually qualified, his co-driver – and therefore

the car – allowed to start by discretion of the organisers. *Vive La France!*

Not so fortunate was the Tiga Volvo. Missing the first day completely, it was all too much for this untried project, Andrew Ratcliffe explaining the chassis was marvellous, only mismatched turbos letting it down. And out, failing to qualify by a substantial margin.

What remained of the grid was the A-team: two Argos, an Alba and a pair of ALDs. Louis Descartes had two BMW-powered beasties, his unraced WRT Audi presumably *Vorsprung durch kaput*, while the might of all Italy could only muster one entry in a race they used to dominate. Techno Racing were upholding national honour although Evan Clements, who survived a frightening moment when the steering broke, was unsure for how long as he commented: "These guys

are smashing, typically Italian, no real organisation, go mad at everything. I think we'll have our lights on, but . . .".

The outlook appeared equally dark to Martin Schanche, the Zakspeed JM19B unusually far back at seventh in class nearly half a minute behind Nick Adams, only a scant few places ahead of his former machine now paraded by Dahm where someone had the most unlikely task of sticking dozens of little coloured strips on plain white bodywork. "Gis a job, I can do that!" Alas such frivolities appeared beyond the humour of Schanche, resigned to disappointment before the race had even started, suggesting the only way he would get a good result was to pray hard. At Lucky Strike all 'a' seemed to stand for was apprehension, anger, alas and *adieu*.

1. The ex-Michael Andretti Royale RP40 was entered by American dragster ace Olindo Jacobelli. 2. The Metaxa Tiga-Cosworth of Los/Wood/Hessert. 3. The Tremblay/Lateste/Boulay ALD 02. 4. The Dahm Argo in the hands of veteran Teddy Pilette. 5. The Ecosses would form up line astern on the grid after an eventful qualifying.

1

1. The pole-grabbing Spice-Hart of the debutant Chamberlain team ahead of the Dianetique Spice Pontiac Fiero DFL. 2. The Roy Baker Racing Tiga GC 286. 3. The Goodmans Bardon qualified on the penultimate row of the grid. 4. Thorkild Thyrring's Tiga GC 287 which was powered by a BDT turbo.

2

3

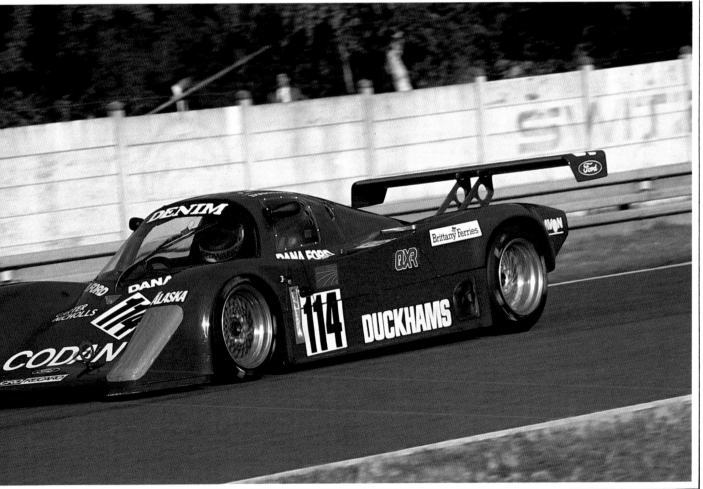

So it was done, qualifying over and the grid set with a whole gamut of emotions from anxiety to zeal shown by those like MSR and Kouros for whom there was fear of the unknown while others such as Spice and Jaguar relished the prospects ahead.

No race that had gone before could possibly act as an indicator of victory, Le Mans being so special, as different, so long as to defy form books. To the uncommitted and the romantic a double celebration for Jaguar and Ecurie Ecosse was their favourite happy ending three decades on from those legends of yore, but La Sarthe is no respecter of tradition nor Hollywood backdrop, tenacity applying here more than tinsel.

The Silk Cats had proven they had both speed and fuel economy capable of victory but nobody could look into a crystal ball to discover their reliability factor. Rothmans Porsche, never idle under the threat, annexed the front row but knew it was not an indicator of any true advantage over their English rivals. They also knew that no amount of testing could replace the knowledge gained by sweat and toil of competition, their greatest asset being hard-earned experience from an unbroken sequence stretching back to 1951, nearly five hundred race entries and eleven victories. Eleven was also the number of 962Cs available to start, with Joest and BLR obvious possibilities for outright honours themselves, others such as Kremer and Obermaier past masters at getting cars home. Porsche could also count on their 961 if the weather turned really foul, a possible trump card in a game of chance, while the Cougar meant aces wild, the Saubers and Japanese jokers in the pack. Twist or bust.

Down in C2, if Ecosse was to keep their date with destiny they would need to overcome not only the abundant speed of both Spice Fieros but the sheer number of Tigas et al. It was not in any way beyond them although in recent years *Les Vingt Quatre Heures* had not been overly sympathetic to their efforts. Like every other competitor out there, the boys from the red stuff would need a prodigious amount of luck to see it through. It

was five stud poker with a pair of aces. Double or quits.

Nobody would give up easily, this race famous for its walking wounded, nowhere else are the vanquished almost as acclaimed as the victors. Ahead lay uncharted territory of a very familiar track, three thousand miles on a road which led nowhere, paving its route to glory for a few and disappointment for many more. As Saturday beckoned each team completed final preparations: discussing strategies, inspecting components, checking everything. The mighty and the minnows all hoping beyond hope nothing had been overlooked, everything humanly possible done to eliminate failure, be it driver error or poor assembly or whatever. But for all their endeavours there was one big question mark hanging over them of which none had any control whatsoever: the weather.

And it was raining. And drizzling. And pouring down. *Il pleut.* When all that stopped it immediately started to rain again. There had been intermittent showers all week, some severe, but this was different with no let up in sight, prospects decidedly unsociable.

Saturday morning spectating became virtually the sole province of Brits well used to vigils in muddy puddles of far off fields that were forever Snet' or Silverstone, the locals having the best idea by mostly staying at home, only Mad Frogs and Englishmen go out in the midday rain.

Everyone was terrified it had settled in for Christmas, the prospect of being out in it for a day-and-a-half decidedly unpleasant – and we weren't driving! Those who were expressed considerable apprehension, terrible conditions sure to increase both danger levels and upset factors quite markedly, morning Warm Up fortunately only confirming the latter where Kouros 62 emerged fastest followed by a Brun Porsche, also Michelin shod.

If Walter could walk on water, and it rain for long periods, then maybe his under-strength team had the stamina within itself to pull off a shock. If the Mercedes V8s would last the distance perhaps they were capable of a sur-

prise. If Herve Regout's thoughts bore fruit we were in for rooster tails of the unexpected. Maybe, perhaps, if . . .

Tom Walkinshaw reacted to such possibilities in his normal laconic style, as assured as anyone could be about his team's ability to cope with the adverse conditions: ". . . everything is going to plan . . . we have just got to race now . . . there are no changes of plans for a wet race . . ." with the threat of French rubber dismissed thus: "I do not know if they are more suitable. I've never had Michelin tyres." Only time would tell and with his cars next quickest during the morning session he had grounds, albeit

soggy ones, for optimism. Should the rain prevail it would be a double edged sword in the battle between Jaguar and Porsche, a consequent slower pace favouring turbo fuel allowances while making them more arduous to drive. It was all building up into one of the most unpredictable Le Mans events for many a long time.

As race time drew ever closer, many traditional festivities washed out by rain, the stadium filled with spectators and anticipation. Whatever distance travelled or language spoken all were embroiled with that same basic curiosity regarding its outcome as last year, the same basic feelings and queries being repeated twelve months further on.

There would be many a private battle fought out in the most public of arenas. There would be success and failure, sadness and joy, for these are the very ingredients, the very essence, of this annual festival of sport and drama. Throughout the circuit, throughout France, throughout the world, people had their own favourites and their own vested interests. There were thousands of questions that would all be answered come this time tomorrow. One question was paramount though: could Jaguar win Le Mans?

BELOW: Designed by Gerard Weltier, the WM P87 had a stylish aerodynamic body that was designed for it to travel at 400 kph (250 mph) on the Mulsanne Straight. It was powered by a twin turbocharged Peugeot V6 engine which was claimed to give 900 bhp. It had a fraught time at the Le Mans Test Days where it was unable to string together two laps. The fastest speed it could achieve in practice was 238 mph and it only qualified 21st on the grid.

THE RACE

It had actually stopped raining as cars came under starter's orders, indeed almost pleasant as the sartorial chic of plastic macs and dustbin liners were discarded, perhaps only temporarily.

Also abandoned for the moment were any expectations of Dorchy and Jacobelli, left behind when the grid set off on two pace laps, Royale 118 refusing to start while WM 52 billowed voluminous clouds of steam. As both were ignominiously pushed towards the sanctuary of pitlane it gave the assembly something to observe as they awaited the first flypast, a Nissan breaking formation to join them, all three destined to make their entrance after the show had started. Around went the Mercedes pace car again, its charges now strung out over a full kilometre, spray still much in evidence as everyone tensed awaiting race start, the dark coupé pulling off at the latest possible moment.

The Rothmans cars accelerated together, hurtling up Pits Straight side by side with all three Jaguars in close attendance although none could find a way past, Hans Joachim easing ahead through the new Dunlop Chicane, Silk Cat 5 dropping behind Kouros 62 and Raphanel's Cougar. Palmer, Thackwell and Larrauri completed this leading bunch, already a gap appearing to Number Seven who was trying hard to fend off the rest, its bright headlamps not due to reflect a day of glory for Joest.

Through the Esses onto Tertre Rouge, Porsche 17 led, all holding station except Brun 2 with whom Oscar slipped inside the Sauber as thirty thousand horsepower was unleashed on that most famous strip of public highway. Down Mulsanne they went, Jochen tacking left with Hanschen a few lengths ahead off his starboard bow until easing across as they entered the Kink, staying there through Mulsanne Corner, Martin Brundle close up, an inspired Johnny Dumfries ready to take Cheever when they reached Porsche Curves. The front group now comprised these five, Jan Lammers slipping back then pitwards as they completed lap one, his wet rubber not practical on a drying surface, Fortuna Brun now sixth, antipodeans Thackwell and Jones next, Cougar splitting the two Toyotas, then Blaupunkt, Raulet's WM, a trio of 962Cs.

The Stuttgart flat six turbo engine also headed C2 with John Cooper's Ivey Tiga clear of Nick Adams and 'Gordy', Mazda 202 spoiling a clean sweep by being next to lead IMSA/GTP while bringing up the rear were both Ecosses, their game plan being specifically to avoid any first lap heroes.

As things turned out there were no calamities on that opening tour despite it being typically fast and furious, nobody ensnared by the new chicane nor changing conditions. Indeed more were caught out by their choice of

RIGHT: The first lap and the leaders swoop down from the famous Dunlop bridge.

footwear, the stops of Lammers then Palmer heralding a spate of early changes. After that they would be in and out like there was no tomorrow – and for some there would not be – the arrivals of Kris Nissen and Sarel van der Merwe having more ominous overtones. They would soon be back . . .

The track was definitely drying out now, Fortuna and Leyton House 962Cs amongst those to stop next time around, the leading trio content to stay out on intermediates, their gap growing ever bigger as Dumfries came in thereby handing his hard won fourth spot back to Cheever, Eddie destined to make his call a lap later.

It was all somewhat chaotic, the incessant comings and goings like a Whitehall Theatre farce, causing mayhem to lap charts and leader boards, the only semblance of good order appearing to be what remained of the front runners. Brundle was now taking the fight to Porsche, splitting them on occasions, Mass having gone ahead down Mulsanne on lap three, his glory to be shortlived, Stuck restoring the status quo as pack leader soon afterwards. With a handful of laps gone these three were already some twenty seconds clear with Toyotas briefly fourth and fifth, Lassig's Porsche following as the other Primagaz

car also stopped, its dreams of a wet race suspended in the animation of off-*piste* activity, much to M. Regout's undoubted disappointment.

Others had decidedly more drastic problems because it was now just before the half hour mark and the Taka-Q car had returned. As it glided pitwards a wisp of white smoke trailed it, a similar symptom also spelling acute distress for Jelinski's Blaupunkt version of the adjacent pit which arrived shortly afterwards although neither compared with Kremer 10, the Yokohama machine doing proud a Papal election. Alas for none of them would there be any miracles or sal-

vation, diagnosis soon indicating they all had blown engines, the cause – disputed by the A.C.O. – being fuel supply and unwise choice of management system microprocessors, the effect being three fewer 962Cs to help Stuttgart fend off those hard charging Jaguars.

Panic and chips à la Porsche, not for many a long day had they suffered such traumas at Le Mans, things getting decidedly worse before they got better when Rothmans 18 reappeared ten minutes after its scheduled pitstop, the factory car now similarly afflicted, sitting forlorn in the pitlane for a while, rejected by one and all. Where-

as the first flurry of activity had regarded tyres a second related to new electronic brains for all Porsches in their quest to avoid any further mishaps, so it was nearly two hours before racing settled down into some sort of rhythm, the blue Rothmans car usually retaining a slender lead over three purple predators with BLR's quasi-962 also ready to pounce. It was all looking good for Britten, for Lloyd, for Britain and Tom Walkinshaw Racing. It was looking good for Jaguar . . .

Not that all the fun and frolics were exclusively C1. Both Argos had long since departed the scene, Fritsch's Porsche-powered example suffering as per Big Brothers while Martin Schanche had no need to concern himself with worrying about his engine, stuffing it into the boonies after only five laps. The Dianetique sponsored Fiero now headed C2, its Hart-powered cousin delayed by more coolant crises, Ecosse close at hand, as always, soon to take over top slot when Fermin Velez suffered a puncture then a split swirl pot, the prelude to a chase through the night for 'Gordy' & Co. Tigas were also showing well, Ivey and Metaxa clear of Dune with Ecosse 101 next up although nearly five laps adrift of team leader Mallock as another drama befell this eventful race, Schaefer crashing his Brun 962C shortly before the three hours mark.

Although not catching fire it had mounted the armco at Maison Blanche much as Price Cobb had done three days earlier, destroying itself and extinguishing another candidate for the crown, a spate of retirements also adding Mazda 201 and Dumfries' Sauber to the 'Liste des Abandons', Johnny setting fastest race lap prior to being replaced by Chip Ganassi upon whom the gearbox broke. Others already out included both WM Peugeots and the Toyotas, Alan Jones getting his wish of an early bath when the pump failed to pick up the last of its fuel as he headed for replenishment. Professional pride apart, you could not help thinking Jonesy would not be too upset . . .

While AJ beat his retreat those who remained had a race to be won or, at least, survived, no more than a dozen in with any reasonable chance of fame and glory beyond being mobile come 16H00 tomorrow. As dusk settled over the Sarthe, a cold grey day giving way to the warmth of sunset, there was an epic duel going on between Porsche and Jaguar, number 17 and the Brundle/Neilsen car diving inside each other through the Esses for lap after lap, side by side along Mulsanne as each strove for supremacy, the other two XJR8-LMs and BLR Porsche usually holding a watching brief as events unfolded before them while Palmer/Weaver/Cobb endeavoured to stay in touch. Gradually, remorselessly Jaguar 6 opened an advantage, eked out to a minute at one point, but Stuck clawing it back as drizzle started to fall, only enough to severely dampen the track to require grooved slicks as they approached the witching hour.

Alan Jones: "I got in as late as I could on Monday and I am getting out as early as I can. The minute the car isn't running I am off like a rocket. As for the result, to be perfectly honest I would not even care about it if I do not read about it in the newspaper. If I am not on the rostrum I do not care who is. This is a profession to me, I don't like the place, I'm only here because of contracts so once my job is finished what happens and who wins is of no concern to me."

1. The Spice Fiero headed the C2 class early in the race.
2. The Ecosses were never far behind. 3. The Toyota suffered a spin. 4. Schaefer crashed the Brun 962C shortly before the 3 hour mark.

Britten Lloyd never got there, Weaver rounding Mulsanne Corner at 23H36 with the car ablaze, an oil union having worked loose, hot liquid spraying onto glowing exhaust pipes with sad results. With only a few items salvageable Richard Lloyd later reported it came within five seconds of *complete* disaster, the fuel tank already blistering when firemen doused the flames. Out of the ashes would rise a phoenix . . .*

Now they were four and in the pits Joest had already cleared away their belongings thereby creating a No Man's Land between adjacent occupied territories of Rothmans Porsche and Silk Cut Jaguar, an unhindered field of vision between the main protagonists, each of whose respective personnel eyed the other with controlled optimism like a pair of wily gunfighters, each believing implicitly himself to be fastest gun in L'Ouest. The only difference being Jaguar had three bullets, Porsche but one. Do not forsake me, oh my darlin'. . .

This was High Midnight, statistics at one third distance showing Stuck/Bell/Holbert with a fifty seconds lead from three Jaguars who were spaced out over only two laps, all well in contention should even the slightest drama befall Porsche 17. Ecosse 102, five laps clear of Spice, was eighth overall, the Tigas were still doing well en masse, the GDBA 962C and private Nissan were recent retirements and Brun's final act was soon to be a failed engine for his Canadians.

Onwards they went through the night, a remorseless blaze of headlamps mixing with the harsh glare of sideshows and beer tents, sounds of parties double tracking with piston engines, only that solitary Mazda rotary different in concept and cadence. Those hours, enveloped in darkness are the essence of Le Mans, its very atmosphere, revelry mixed with racing, only participants unable to enjoy the ambience as they prepare for a long Sunday.

The commentators' tannoys provide a link with the outside world for those who never get to see beyond the retaining wall, interspersed pop music haunting senses in those quieter mo-

ments when the Pit Straight is empty, every note resonating around whitened walls until engulfed by the urgent cry of a passing racecar.

The terraces and grandstands had become much emptier now, only the Pits Balcony still containing an unbroken wall of faces, each one eager to glimpse down upon contenders as they

went about their business, pace virtually undiminished by any lateness of hour, pitwork as critical as ever. At the unfashionable end of proceedings Vêtir could be seen fixing their ill-functioning lights system, unaware the engine would cruelly expire just after dawn; ALD had a rear suspension in pieces, their painstaking endeavours

*The car would re-appear at the next SP-WC round in Germany two weeks later and win the event!

not proving in vain.

Suddenly the tempo sped up and tension mounted as a phalanx of flash-guns announced the arrival of Roth-mans 17, Derek Bell replacing Hans Stuck behind the wheel, new tyres for old, another twenty gallons safely aboard. The well drilled routine was precisely that, Porsche crews having untold hours of experience at these things, the only aspect outside their control being choice of accompanying music, Dire Straits' 'Brothers In Arms' blending Mark Knofler's guitar and vocals with their air drills and jack hammers, the leading car en route again before the last verse is over, synthesiser fused with syncromesh.

1. The Britten Lloyd car shortly before it caught fire and was almost totally destroyed. 2. The private Nissan ran midfield in the race before being caught out in an accident around midnight.

1. The Canadian Porsche reached ninth place before it was out with engine failure. Night time pit stops for: 2, 3. the Vetir Tiga to adjust their ill-functioning lighting system; 4. the ALD to rectify the suspension; 5. the Chamberlain Spice making a scheduled stop.

5

'Through these fields of destruction, baptism of fire' . . . Jaguar maintained their vigil through the darkest hours, Porsche maintained their advantage, hoping for some respite to slow the pace in order to help a critical fuel allowance, Coventry having four star in abundance. It came just before three o'clock. Win Percy had taken over the Lammers/Watson car for his first stint when it turned right at the Kink, striking armco barriers at some 200 mph, barrel-rolling into oblivion. Suddenly there was an extra chill in the cold night air, the cataclysm of violence searing not only metal and carbon fibre but the nerves of those awaiting news. Tired faces took on a whole new dimension, expressions anxious not to show any signs of inner turmoil or emotion, only frightened wide eyes betraying their worst fears, many unable to exorcise the haunting spectre of Jo Gartner's accident a year ago . . .

When the news came through it was all good, the affable and popular West Countryman miraculously unscathed by his ordeal, only the cockpit and V12 remaining of Jaguar 5; wheels, gearbox, windscreen, doors etc. jettisoned in flight. Three layer armco had restrained the XJR8-LM from ploughing into trees beyond, the almost full fuel tanks intact . . . 'I have witnessed your suffering, as the battle raged higher'.

"It was only my third lap. We think it picked up some debris at the Porsche Curves, others did, and going down through the Esses someone said the car bottomed more than normal although I did not notice anything.

"Just before the Kink, I was doing 6500 rpm (approx 200 mph/320 kph), it started buffeting badly and something went off. It was obviously the rear tyre. Whether it took off part of the rear bodywork I do not know, all I know is that immediately, without any wrench of the steering wheel, it suddenly veered right, straight into the armco at forty-five degrees. From then on it was a case of barrel rolls and flying, the doors came off, my helmet almost ground through.

"You don't have time to get frightened, you think of survival. I pulled my knees up and arms in. I wanted to remain conscious which was all that concerned me. Once, when I was flying, it came down quite heavily and I just felt like relaxing, letting it all go, thinking I couldn't pull in for much longer, then something inside you says not to be stupid, keep your arms in, keep your legs up and you fight for consciousness. The biggest fear is fire and what you don't want is to be trapped in a burning car. I remained conscious, the car stopped and I undid the belts, looked up the road, nothing coming, ran across, jumped the armco and sat down. I was very, very lucky.

"I am told it was the most spectacular and fastest accident, the only one at that place and spced where the driver has walked away from it. Two factors are most important, the first is how strong the car was, how safety conscious the team are because the fuel cells were virtually full and there was no rupture at all and, secondly, the three layer armco at the Kink. A combination of those things saved my life . . .

. . . Apparently it is on Breakfast Television tomorrow. Marvellous isn't it, all the years I have been racing and nobody wanted to know. Go and write something off in a big way . . ."

There was now a ceasefire, a lull in proceedings while armco was repaired and debris cleared, Silk Cats licking their wounds while Porsche savoured some cream having gained a vital advantage: two hours of pace cars. And it was now only two against one with the Obermaier/Primagaz 962C fourth, the pendulum beginning to swing away from Kidlington for the first time all week . . . Not that the period became good news for all, Ecosse 101 stopping on Mulsanne with a flat battery, Mike Wilds having to wait again for his first Sarthe finish. Meanwhile a batch of Tigas still followed the dogged resistance of Mallock/Leslie/Duez to Spice/Velez/de Henning from afar.

Onwards they went, dawn breaking to reveal Porsche with a lead of about ninety seconds, thick mist shrouding Mulsanne as Brundle/Neilsen continued their quest with pace cars withdrawn, Cheever/Boesel usually two laps adrift as they endeavoured to make up eight minutes lost to throttle-linkage difficulties, time which meant the difference between first and third, delight or defeat. They were then further delayed when Boesel slid wide at Arnage, damaging the nose, loosening still further Jaguar's grip on the Holy Grail, acting as a prelude to a spate of dramas which over the next two hours would effectively seal the outcome of this hard fought race.

The biggest of two near simultaneous calamities was the loss of Jaguar 6, Neilsen coming in with a cracked cylinder head around breakfast time, the car which had been at the forefront of TWR's bid for victory now vanquished, its engine cooked, pushed away into honourable retirement. Although Cheever/Boesel were promoted into second spot they were now nearly four laps adrift and it was all looking bad for Jaguar.

Things became worse soon afterwards. Although blameless, Eddie severely damaged the gearbox when he inadvertently selected reverse, effectively doing the same to Jaguar progress and any lingering hopes of winning. Initial and subsequent repair stops lost some fifteen laps, about an hour of track time, thus giving Porsche the final cushion they needed as Number 17 serenely reeled off lap after lap, its job all but done. For sure it could break but somehow everyone knew it wouldn't . . .

1. The Lammers/Watson/Percy Jaguar was out before dawn broke when an horrific accident befell the car. 2. Ecosse Number 101 succumbed to a flat battery on the Mulsanne Straight during the night and was out.

Derek Bell (08H40 Sun): "I knew the Jags were having a few problems. Boesel overtook me then threw rubbish all over my car so I knew he wasn't going to last long in front of me . . . It's like an ice rink out there now . . ."

The two protagonists still fought it out on the Sunday, but by breakfast Porsche had broken the back of the Jaguar onslaught.

As mechanics toiled to get Jaguar 6 mobile again there were all the exasperations of dreams broken and marketing ploys erased, performances unrewarded and P.R. scoops scuppered. With feet firmly on the ground Messrs Walkinshaw and Silman stood behind their surviving charge already planning for twelve months hence while in the dugout Jan Lammers – who had also done a stint in the car – looked forlorn as he awaited any further instructions, a hard night's day

breaking in vain. On high, Sir John Egan peered down from his hospitality suite, head in hands, heavy of heart. Next time, they vowed, next time.

This time Primagaz were the main beneficiaries of Jaguar woes, the Obermaier 962C of Lassig/Yver/de Dryver briefly second until the XJR regained its stride, retaking it when the Coventry carnivore was again reduced to a purple pussycat around lunchtime by fuel pressure and suspension problems. Meanwhile the

similarly liveried Primagaz Cougar had overcome the early dramas of fuel pump action to stage a superb dice with its stablemate, the five laps lost on Saturday night due to be crucial by race finish.

Now it was Sunday morning and for many it became a fight for survival as much as anything, one which Nissan failed to meet as their final hope succumbed to engine breakage, the sun not quite setting on Japanese honour as the Euro-Mazda continued

to circulate, all threats to class victory finally ending in a blaze of non-glory after Nierop whacked the Indianapolis barriers with the Porsche 961, its burnt out wreck disgorging a large number of undamaged data recording systems.

In C2 yellow closed remorselessly on red, Ecosse powerless to deny Gordon Spice after a spell of early morning sickness, mostly transmission related, kept the sole remaining Swift-air machine stationary for extended periods, a cherished victory not about

to be delivered by the Anglo-Scots enterprise. For Charles Ivey the time at rest would be forever, Tiga Porsche 123 breaking its crankshaft when a clear third in class, heartbreak after eighteen hours. As morning became afternoon their story would be echoed by Dune, less than two-and-a-half hours left when their Metro V6 cried enough, the Alba outlasting Evan Clements' prediction but not the allotted time.

1. As the surviving Jaguar is in the pits on Sunday morning with yet more trouble, a studious Tom Walkinshaw and a tired Roger Silman look on. 2. John Egan, meanwhile, ponders the team's misfortune with resignation. 3. The Obermaier 962C of Lassig/Yver/de Dryver steals second place while the Jaguar is in the pits. 4. A fairly dishevelled Cougar nevertheless continues to finish in third place. 5. The Porsche 961 fails to finish when Nierop crashed it into the barriers at Indianapolis.

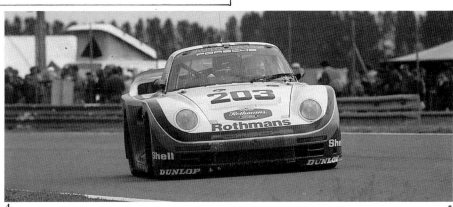

3

4

5

1

2

1. The C2 class winning Spice Fiero. 2. The Charles Ivey Tiga-Porsche broke a crankshaft when it was a clear third in class. 3. The Alba also failed to finish despite surviving the night.

As those final hours ticked away it was not all tears and sadness, Kremer well pleased to get Foucha/Franz Konrad/Wayne Taylor into fourth place as recompense for the early departure of their other entry, ALD ecstatic to finish both of their cars in formation despite a myriad of earlier problems. Hugh Chamberlain was undoubtedly similarly relieved, his Spice Hart very swift when running well but unable to make up the deficit of those early misfortunes, Tiga finally getting two finishers after the latter stages proved too much for their peer group.

Alas, the last few moments were all too much for the Bassaler Sauber. Held at the pitlane exit ready to complete those last two vital laps to qualify as a finisher it could not make the grade, the gentle slope defeating its clutch, rolling back from whence it came, the cheers of encouragement from spectators not proving enough to assist its progress.

The biggest displays of audience participation continued to be opposite *chez* Jaguar, a twenty four hours' vigil having greeted every arrival and departure with rapturous applause, those after extended stoppages notably more

so. Now with the race truly lost they continued their task undaunted, a lonely fifth place no reason for despondency, each lap accompanied by a crescendo of noise and banner waving, each pitstop an excuse for 'You'll Never Walk Alone' and 'Rule Brittania'. A few idiots aside, if TWR could harness their energy it would probably be worth about five seconds a lap . . .

Primagaz also had plenty to shout about, second and third beyond their wildest dreams, Obermaier's steady run proving well rewarded while Yves Courage could not contain his excitement at becoming a local boy made

good, his Cougar the pride of the city, the pride of France. Others with reasons to celebrate were Spice and Mazdaspeed, sixth and seventh overall besides winning their respective categories, the Fiero only four laps away from ousting Jaguar while the 757 recorded the highest ever finish for Japan. One day . . .

Today belonged to Derek Bell, Hans Stuck and Al Holbert, Their victory had been supreme, won by a cohesion of factors not least of which were superbly modulated driving and excellent reliability when the odds against them often seemed far higher than the three-to-one situation prevalent during much of the event. Indeed, Jaguar had been defeated as much by inexperience as circumstance, the Coventry marque again vowing to return with avengence. No prize they win can ever compare with the continued good health of Winston Percy.

As the three drivers took their accolades amongst the chaos and mayhem of that traditional champagne rostrum ceremony they did so as a repeat of the previous encounter, returned to power by a huge majority. It was an emphatic win for the blue team. Just like the General Election.

1. Porsche Number 17 takes the chequered flag thus according a most satisfying win for the Stuttgart team. 2. The surviving Jaguar coming home fifth is nevertheless accorded a hero's welcome by its many fans there.

2

1. The winning Porsche had fans all of its very own. 2. Stuck, Holbert and Bell on the winner's rostrum, a repeat of 1986. 3. Mr. Petitjean of Primagaz is flanked by the second and third place drivers, all sponsored by Primagaz.

An XJR-5 was classified a finisher in '85, the Group 44 machine staggering around a final couple of laps on eleven cylinders after spending much of Sunday afternoon in the pits. Prior to that, the last Jaguar to complete the 24 Hours was in 1963, Richards and Grossman bringing home Briggs Cunningham's E-type '5115 WK' in ninth place after a variety of troubles.

As this year sees the farewell to the Ford Capri it is worth recording that two three litre RS 2600s finished tenth and eleventh in the 1972 race. So next year, whip out the furry dice . . .

It was twenty years ago today . . . the Chaparrals came to play, only to fall by the wayside. This made it another Ferrari v. Ford confrontation, the All-American team of Dan Gurney and A. J. Foyt bringing their seven litre Mk IV home 32 miles ahead of the Scuderia's best effort.

Jackie Stewart's only Le Mans was in 1965, sharing the Rover BRM turbine to tenth place with Graham Hill.

Is 1964 winner Jean Guichet the most 'unfamous' victor ever? His twelve participations include second in '61, third a year later plus leading in '65. His final race netted fifth in 1969, fittingly with Nino Vaccarella his partner aboard the Ferrari 275P five years earlier.

The first Porsche entered at Le Mans was for local drivers Veuillet and Mouche in 1951. Their 1100cc type 356 came home twentieth, the next year eleventh. It was to be the start of something big . . .

Brun's most exciting moment came on Wednesday evening. As a mechanic stooped to glance at the right rear tyre the engine started, a long flame shooting from those nearby exhausts to singe his moustache. Everyone else thought it was funny!

It was incorrectly reported that Thomas Hibbert ran all the way back from Mulsanne to the pits for tools with which to repair his stranded GP/Cosmik Tiga on Saturday night. A car is officially deemed to have been abandoned if the driver goes more than ten metres from it. One small step for Tom, one giant leap for Metaxa.

Some enterprising individual was trying to sell not naughty French postcards but some photostatted details of an apparently new C2 challenger, the Schnitzer-BMW powered Duplex DB02. It beats trying to raise sponsorship!

Roger Silman quoted a total of eighty-eight people for TWR. There were seventy-two 'staffers' directly involved with car prep, six Mulsanne Corner signallers and no shortage of willing helpers.

At last it happened. Someone finally fell off the pitlane balcony, collecting ex-McLaren and Ensign chief mechanic Gary Anderson on his way down. Fortunately Gary, who was assisting Spice Engineering, is a big strong lad – having been known to pick up a DFV unaided! – and recovered well from his injuries. When will they ever learn?

How long before someone, race driver or supposed 'enthusiast', is killed in the mayhem of race finish. They now run across the track *before* 4 p.m.! Utter madness!

The prize for sartorial elegance must go to Graham Duxbury. Were you aware that winkle-picker shoes were back in fashion? You betcha . . .

The excellent third place by Cougar is the first time a non-Porsche chassis has finished in the top five at Le Mans since Group C began. Likewise, by way of consolation, Jaguar's fifth place is the highest non-Porsche engine in the same period. Next year. . .

What a great pity that Kouros do not see fit to spend less on the hype and Hooray-Henris, more on Peter Sauber's fabulous cars . . .

Although Jaguar fans were the most conspicuous all week, Porsche were not without their support. One banner, all in German, hailed the 'finkenwerden'. So now you know . . .

Amongst a myriad of information supplied by the A.C.O. were technical details of all participating vehicles. It is very interesting to note that 'chassis' in the French version was translated into the Anglais edition as 'undercarriage'. Chocks away!

Rothmans press releases at Le Mans advised recipients to contact a Cambridge office if further info was required. Upon doing so only two days after the race, your intrepid reporter was redirected by a telephone operator to a St. Ives number where someone stated that all matters were now handled direct from Rothman's HQ in Aylesbury. What a good job for them the racing team is not run in similar fashion . . .

In twenty eight Le Mans starts since 1976, WM have only once scored a top ten finish: fourth in '80 with Roger Dorchy and Guy Frequelin.

Tom Walkinshaw raced at Le Mans five times as a driver between 1976 and '82, failing to finish on any occasion.

The forty-eight starters this year meant the second lowest number since the event resumed in 1949, only '69 with 45 being lower.

Johnny Dumfries' fastest lap was only the second by a non-Porsche in the last ten events, Ragnotti's Rondeau being equally successful in 1982.

The annual press conference was a very illuminating affair even for those of us who do not parlez le lingo; one most fascinating aspect being the heated exchange between Bob Wollek – French *and* on pole position – and those six wise men of the top table, whose apparent responses pleading poverty were not accepted by the crowd at large. Apropos money there was also lots more shoulder shrugging around frequent use of the phrase 'le business de Monsieur Ecclestone'. Need one know more. . .?

97

Porsche's seventh consecutive victory beats the straight six of Ferrari between 1960/65.

Luigi Chinetti is the only previous winner ever to be honoured as official race starter, in 1982. Wouldn't it be nice if they were to allow Phil Hill or Jacky Ickx that same accolade.

Le Mans stalwarts missing from action this year for various reasons included previous winners Klaus Ludwig and Paolo Barilla, the ever unlucky Brian Redman and Hans Meyer, Jean Louis Schlesser, British privateer Alain de Cadenet and Claude Ballot Lena, the veteran Frenchman finally breaking a run of 21 consecutive appearances, his best result being third in a Porsche 935 some ten years ago . . .

No bikini clad Hawaiian Tropic girlies this year. Aaah! The Silk Cut lovelies with long legs and puffball skirts could not compare while most visually stunning were those Toyota ladies adorned in traditional kimonos and porcelain expressions. Exquisite.

If Fermin Velez is the smallest driver around, then George Fouche is surely the biggest, his build seemingly more suitable for Twickenham than Tertre Rouge.

In the book 'Presse Informations' pop drummer Slim Borgudd is listed as a 'batteur de rock'. Rock on, Tommy!

Interestingly Porsche 17 completed 174 laps during the first twelve hours while fighting off those Tom Cats, then 180 during the second half as competition fell away . . .

All the first four cars home were on a different make of rubber: Dunlop, Goodyear, Michelin and Yokohama respectively with sixth-first in C2 going going to Avon. Only Bridgestone missed out, neither Nissan nor Toyota making the chequered flag.

When was the last time a driver notched up fastest lap on his first every visit to Le Mans? Johnny Dumfries did.

Hands up all those who reckon the Sauber Mercedes to be the prettiest car around. Is it because it actually has proper wheel arches: and then there is *that* sound . . .

Porsche's winning margin of twenty laps represents 270 kms, the second largest margin of all time, beaten only by the race sixty years ago when the Benjafield/Davis Bentley finished 350 kms ahead of a Salmson.

Dune Motorsport had a sign on one of their tents in Le Village. Some wag transposed the first and third letters of their name . . .

A straw poll of listeners seemed to categorise the efforts of Radio Le Mans as 'tries hard, could do better' but undoubtably *the* star of Le Mans

'87 was Bob Constanduros. Great stuff!

Scott Goodyear had never seen Le Mans nor driven a 962C before race week. Three days after La Sarthe he was due to undertake an Indycar rookie test. Quite a learning curve!

There was plenty of evidence of 'Ferrari Formula'; the new clock, at the press conference etc. What a pity there was no evidence of any Ferrari Group C Racing cars . . .

Weren't some, a few, of those supposed Jag fans grotesque: their behaviour a discredit and insult to all. Drunken slobs who were 'mooning' – and worse – at the end of the race need a good kick up the . . .

Three guesses as to who owns the Porsche 956 with which he won the '83 Le Mans? Answers on a postcard to . . .

As the race entered its final phase, the surviving Jaguar in a lonely fifth place, Tom Walkinshaw is reported to have told his drivers to enjoy their Sunday drive and admire the daffodils . . .

If nothing else, the Bardon must have won any prize for most sponsored car. It was smothered in differing names.

How do you know when you have got back to Blighty? Surely by the traffic cones. There were six major sets between Dover and the Dartford Tunnel whereas nearly a thousand miles in France had been cone free . . .

Klaus Ludwig missed Le Mans on safety grounds then raced a Sierra Cosworth a fortnight later in the Nürnburgring 24 Hours – around the *old* circuit! In fact he won, covering 3737 kms of the twisty track – an equivalent of 254 laps of the Sarthe.

There was panic *chez* Bardon when Robin Donovan discovered he had forgotten to bring his competitions licence.

What a pity nobody sees fit to have red, white and blue 'sun strips' on the three Jags. Very patriotic.

The nearest Rothmans Porsche 17 came to mechanical dramas during the race was a duff battery which needed to be changed during the night. Their only other little hiccup related to a

loose windscreen that needed to be taped in place. What a good job they had the men from Autoglass around!

Why don't they make Le Mans worth, say, fifty points towards the WS-PC title? Surely its stature and duration warrant more than a quick thrash around Jarama or that even less time-consuming run about the Noris-ring . . .

Derek Bell is now only one win behind Jacky Ickx in the Sarthe's overall Hall of Fame. Using WS-PC points system he trails the Belgian by 165 to 145 – just that vital sixth success keeping them apart – although using GP additions the score is 72 and 60 respectively. Ickx started fifteen times while Dinger has been around on seventeen occasions.

They changed course at Le Mans again. Last year the reprofiled Mulsanne Corner was well accepted by all but this time the new Dunlop Chicane received more mixed reaction. Following on from a similar venture at Silverstone it was interesting to discover driver reactions:

Henri Pescarolo: "It is interesting. You have quick cars on the track with slow cars coming from the pits which will be a problem, especially at night."

Hans Stuck: "It is not necessary but it is not too bad. There are much worse chicanes: like Hockenheim or the new Silverstone one which is useless and bad to drive. At least this is good to drive."

Graham Duxbury: "A total waste of time! It is not as bad as the new Silverstone chicane but it is not as nice as the old corner where you could sweep over the top."

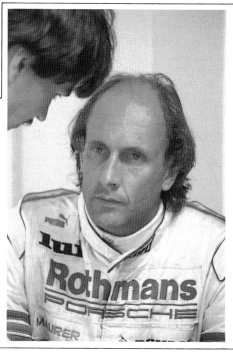

OLD HANDS, NEW FACES

Every year Le Mans brings together the disparity of experience and novelty; those to whom the Sarthe has long ceased to be a stranger whereas newcomers include some whose first glimpse of this daunting place was after scrutineering. It's too late to turn back then! The opportunity was taken to seek out some of these heroes and ask them about their early memories and/or initial impressions. Read into them what you will:

Derek Bell: "My first race here was in 1970 with Ronnie Peterson in a 'works' Ferrari 512 which blew up on Mulsanne after a couple of hours. I thought they would give us the big 'Team Manager' bit but there were no tactics at all which was ridiculous to people who were just F1/F2 drivers . . . There was a big crash right in front of me coming through White House when Reine Wisell was going from side to side, his windscreen co-

vered in oil, trying to see. Regazzoni hit him (Mike Parkes was also involved in this notorious accident) and I remember seeing lots of flames in my mirrors. As I passed the pits everyone was looking down the road and missed me so when I walked in after abandoning the car they thought I had been involved in the accident which I hadn't."

Hurley Heywood: "I won in 1977 which was my first time here! It was in a Porsche 936 with Jurgen Barth when Jacky Ickx joined us after his own had retired. We were well back then and he drove brilliantly. My '83 win was much more gratifying as we *all* had to work very hard."

David Leslie: "The first time I drove the Mulsanne was in 1984. When I got down there my knuckles were white from hanging on to the thing, the original Ecosse. As you get used to it you aren't so tense so now I can go flat

out all the way, take a breather in the middle, read off the gauges and wave to the British marshalls' post. It is now a lot easier than the first time – I soon discovered how quick 200 mph really was!"

Johnny Dumfries: "I never judge a circuit on its straight as it is easy to drive down a straight. The most challenging part of this track is the Porsche Curves. As for night driving I did my quickest qualifying time then so it speaks for itself . . ."

Vern Schuppan: "My first time was in 1973 in a Mirage (with John Watson and Mike Hailwood) running third or so at about one o'clock in the morning when I turned it over at Tertre Rouge. I had just refuelled! Someone had slid wide and spread fine gravel over the corner and it was nothing more than a simple spin but I went into the armco at an angle, it tipped back and launched the car . . ."

Mike Thackwell: "This is my third time and if you don't like it you don't come here. It is a stupid and dangerous race – a team and reliability trial really – but holds a fascination as it has a lot of history. When it stops most people (drivers, teams) will say 'great' but while it continues drivers like myself will keep coming back."

Henri Pescarolo: "My first race was in 1966 and the beginning of a fantastic story with Matra which stays vivid in my memory – not just the first one. I raced here seven times for them, winning three."

Graham Duxbury: "I drove here two years ago with Danner and Capelli in the March when we only just finished. This car (the Spice Hart) handles properly although maybe not as quick in a straight line. The March was a pig! At the end of twenty four hours I was very happy it was all over . . ."

Hans Stuck: "My first time was in 1972 in a Capri (with Jochen Mass) but it did not last long, the engine broke. The next year I was with Chris Amon in a BMW and sleeping in the bus while he drove. All of a sudden I woke up and found him lying next to me. I thought 'Aaahh! Good Heavens! Chris Amon!' 'but it was okay, we were already out. All the rest were rubbish until I came to Porsche . . . It is much easier to drive a powerful car like the 962 as very few cars overtake you. In a slower car it is very difficult to watch the traffic."

John Neilsen: "Everyone remembers my crash in the Sauber in 1984, the photographs are quite dramatic (Indeed they are!). I went down the straight, just sitting there steering, when the thing suddenly took off like an aeroplane and I realised I was flying. I thought 'something has happened . . . there must be a bang now'. It took a long time to hit the ground that first time and, luckily, it landed on its wheels . . . After that it took me ten or fifteen laps to go flat over the little hill there. My brain said to go flat but every time my foot lifted. It is not a problem any more . . ."

Kris Nissen: "It is a great place. I do not think it is as dangerous as some people say or only because of the circuit. If this were a normal 1000 kms race there would be less accidents. I'm not too worried, I am in a good car . . . I was here at the Tests and went through the Kink flat on my third lap. I do not think it is a big problem . . . I have talked to a lot of people: Mr Kremer, Neilsen, Stuck, Mass about what to do, where to be careful . . ."

Andrew Ratcliffe: "I finally got to go down the Mulsanne. I was nervous but the speed did not worry me. We ran down at 200 mph plus a couple of times – it was marvellous – while other times it would be in second gear trying to stay out of everybody's way, praying a lot. This was at night time in the rain . . ."

Herve Regout: "I drove a Ferrari 512BB in 1980 and '82, a converted road car. The Mulsanne was hard work at 320 kph so when I came back in '85 in the Obermaier 956 I thought 350 kph was going to be *very* hard work. My first lap was at night and I was flat – so easy!"

Scott Goodyear: "I had never even seen the track before this week and I love it. I am used to it now (23H55, Saturday) and now know where I am going which is much more of a help . . ."

Ian Harrower, from Wandsworth, competed in his ninth Le Mans 24 Hours, but not with his usual Brentford-based A.D.A. team. Due to lack of sponsorship and time to complete its new car, A.D.A. withdrew its entry for this year's classic. It appeared that Ian would be unable to continue his run of consecutive appearances at the event, and thus not have the chance of repeating last year's success when the A.D.A. team won the C2 category and came eighth overall.

However, at the last moment, he was offered the chance to drive with Kingston dentist, John Sheldon, and Dane, Thorkild Thyrring, in a works C2 Tiga. This car had a turbocharged 2.1 litre Ford engine, his first experience of turbo-power, being more used to the normally aspirated Grand Prix Ford Cosworth engine.

Problems with the engine in practice were rectified for the race, but the apparent cure introduced a new problem: the turbo was 'blowing' fuel past the piston rings and mixing with the oil, diluting it. The oil pressure warning light came on during Ian's first driving stint, some 2½ hours into the race. As a precaution therefore, the engine oil was syphoned off at every pit stop and replaced, thereby losing the team considerable time. In all, 120 litres of Duckhams was used during the race!

This was the major problem for the team, although driving in the wet on dry tyres at night, with no windscreen wiper, had also to be endured by the drivers!

The Tiga Ford car finally finished this gruelling event in 10th position overall and fourth in the C2 category.

TOP CAT

It was a bunch of flowers which made the difference. Do not ask me what they were for I have no idea, being one of those who consider gardening as nothing a bag of cement cannot cure. Nonetheless, they sure looked the part . . .

Delicately arranged in a little white vase atop a low partition, there be a reception and dining area beyond although most attention was inevitably drawn to the outer sanctum complete with wall-to-wall carpet, the warmth emanating from its red hue a far cry from those cold and bare floors of adjacent premises.

Neither the best restaurant in town nor those fine, upstanding offices of the A.C.O., this was Le Village, home for a week to the canvas garages of motorsport and on that carpet, in front of that vase, there sat a 220 mph sports prototype ready for action. A Cougar Porsche C20.

It belonged to the man who had travelled least far to join this throng, Yves Courage being a thirty-nine year old Porsche and Mitsubishi dealer with premises in Boulevard de Morieux on the other side of town. It is now over twenty years since he started in motorsport, undertaking a Jim Russell course at Magny Cours before venturing out in a Gordini then acquiring an ex-Jacques Laffite Formula Renault although his main thrust of the Seventies became hillclimbs with over eighty wins aboard a wide variety of Formula Two machinery.

While his marque title is an anagram of a suitable surname, when he first undertook to participate at Le Mans in 1972 contemporary reports mistook it for a pseudonym. Sharing Barry Robinson's Chevron B21 with its owner and Jean Rondeau – Yves now endeavouring to emulate those subsequent successes of his fellow Sarthois – unfortunately he was not destined to race as a series of cylinder head problems caused delays then early retirement. Five years later he returned, since then missing only one event (1979) and undismayed at not having finished higher than eighteenth. Until now.

As Group C regulations were finally confirmed by FISA in June of 1981 Project cougar was launched, the stylish coupé designated CO1 debuting at Nurburgring a year later, its aluminium monocoque built by that Vichy based English miracle man Don Foster: powered by a Cosworth DFV, tyres by Dunlop, driving entrusted to Courage, Jean Phillipe Grand and former Ensign GP man Patrick Gail-

liard. Although it attracted much attention sadly not all was for the right reasons, a lack of testing evident when qualifying twenty-third with incorrect gearing then lasting only a single race lap before broken suspension ended their day.

Next came Le Mans, a 3.3 litre DFL now installed, Michel Dubois sitting in for Gailliard yet despite some concentrated testing their new car problems persisted with Cougar 35 succumbing as the sun rose on Sunday morning. Only on its third outing, at Spa in September, did C01 finally see a chequered flag, albeit last by some considerable margin after hub problems intervened, Nick Faure and Herve Regout – his first outing with Cougar – sharing honours with Yves Courage.

As a learning year it had been arduous, 1983 to prove likewise with a solitary run at Le Mans lasting less time than their inaugural venture, CO1 now in B-spec and sporting Michelin tyres, unable to make the engine go beyond half distance. There would be two more outings for the car,

1. Yves Courage. 2, 3. Third place for the team at Le Mans was a great reward for the little team from France.

early in '84, before being replaced by CO2 in time for Le Mans but a new chassis failed to bring better luck and the Cougar was already long gone when champagne started to flow from the victory rostrum. Subsequently used in America for IMSA racing, almost immediately work began to start on another new design, designation CI2.

Whereas both previous examples had utilised a ubiquitous Cosworth V8 this new challenger represented a totally different approach: Porsche 956 flat six turbo unit allied to Weissach's own transmission yet suspended by local interest. Initially tested by quadruple Sarthe champion Henri Pescarolo – who would subsequently race it at Spa – the latest model proved consistent with much French thinking apropos the race when it blasted down RN 138 at a phenomenal 371 kph, this 'Mulsanne Special' unable to better nineteenth on the grid, its race progress hindered by a couple of trips dans le undergrowth, almost an hour lost patching the wounds, twentieth little

reward. But at least it had finished.

As per 1986, eighteenth place for the much revised machine after losing a door then nearly five hours manufacturing a replacement. Without such dramas it would have been an open and shut case to finish inside the top ten, the CI2 running unimpaired with a full compliment of panels.

Needless to say, a better type of door fixing is employed on the new 1987 Cougar, the C20. Although superficially similar to earlier examples all aerodynamics have been subtely revised by development engineer Marcel Hubert, the man who's name first came to prominence with victory in 1978, Pironi and Jaussaud doing the honours for La Belle France aboard their Renault Alpine, while another former employee of the Regie, Alain Touchais, is responsible for developing suspension and chassis, the latter penned by Jean Claude Rose.

Considerably more of an all round performer than previous models, the C20 first appeared at Monza in April where despite a lack of prior testing

they qualified eleventh then finished ninth having spent a lot of time repairing suspension damaged by a wayward C2. Ninth; those two points represented Cougar's first ever score in a WEC/WS-PC event. Perhaps things were looking up for Yves Courage, although with an ironic twist of fate it was the only time he had not raced his own car since starting the Cougar story . . .

Silverstone did not add an enthralling chapter, out early with broken transmission, team spirits were soon back in top gear when Pierre Henri Raphanel recorded fourth best lap during the Le Mans Test Day one week later, also being fastest down the shute at 229 mph.

It was a prelude to glory for all at Cougar, their C20 outqualified only by those factory Porsches and Jaguars, lining up in sixth place as best of the rest.

Twenty four hours later it would not only be in his team's paddock sanctuary where you would find bouquets and red carpet for Yves Courage.

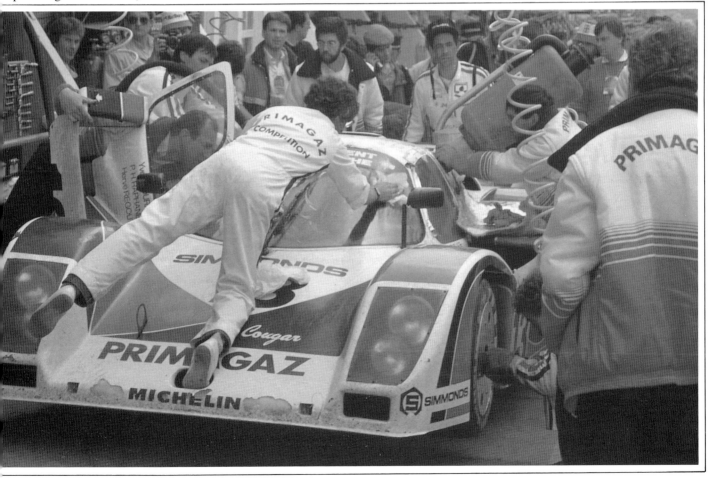

ONE NIGHT IN DUNE

"I am devastated," announced a weary Duncan Bain, turning away to the sanctity of the pitlane dugout, his shoulders which were held so high only a few hours before now slumped low, weighed down by the tiredness of a long night and the gall of bitter disappointment.

The venture had started in optimistic mood but, like the weather, had fluctuated as fortunes ebbed and flowed throughout the week that is Le Mans, the washed out sunshine of Sunday lunchtime not enough to dispel the rain in the hearts of Bain, his partner Neil Crang, nor the rest of that happy band which embraces Dune Motorsport.

Team Managed by John McNeil, he and his mechanics veterans of a disastrous foray with Tim Lee Davey last year, this time they were ready for the fray, the new Tiga GC287 having debuted at Monza, albeit briefly, then run to the flag at Silverstone where the proprietors had been joined by Swiss hillclimb champion Jean Krucker ready for their three handed assault on le mont de la Sarthe.

All knew it would be uphill all the way, their superbly prepared car – sufficiently so to win the coveted Concours d'Elegence prize from the scrutineers ahead of those Jaguars and Porsches et al – having but a single engine at its disposal, the amputation of Austin Rover's motorsport arm not having released sufficient parts to build a back up unit they so desperately needed. No spare, no second chance. The solitary source of power was a Metro V6, similar to that used by Ecosse to win the C2 Teams' title last term, now bored out to 3200cc, Sam Nelson's name replacing Terry Hoyle on the cam covers. Capable of over 400bhp and 9000rpm for 'conventional' enduros, the drivers would be restricted to 330bhp/7250rpm in anticipation of surviving the 24 Hours.

They whould be so lucky! Wednesday's qualifying sessions were bedevilled by a persistent misfire, mocking their efforts and making it impossible for the Tiga to roar at more than 5000rpm, only Duncan having any opportunity of a clear lap, his time sufficient to nett fifth in class and thirty-third overall.

Throughout the following day they beavered away to discover the cause of their misfortunes, furrowed brows much in evidence, Bain commenting: "It has been quite competitive but we have got a gremlin in the management system which is proving to be elusive. We only did about seven laps yesterday before picking up the misfire so Neil and Jean still have to qualify. They cannot possibly do so as it is now, so we have to make other arrangements if necessary, possibly to get them qualified in another car."

As the day wore on the sands of time were running out for Dune

1. Neil Crang looks on as the car is worked on during a troubled practice. 2. The car is pushed through the paddock to the interest of onlookers. 3. The car circulated well and inherited third place in C2.

Motorsport, the nightmare of another failure to qualify hanging over John McNeil like the Hounds of Hades ready to devour any who fell by the wayside. Closer and closer came the hour of reckoning until finally their troubles were traced to a faulty rotor arm, this recalcitrate object shorting out those ever-so-important micro-chips which form the very brain of Lucas' Micos management system. Once cured the V6 burst into life, firing up the hopes of all, its melodious free running sound a veritable symphony after the discord of that misfire.

There were no further dramas during practice, only the elements against them as both Crang and Krucker recorded their qualifying times, a few seconds slower than Bain, the Tiga slipping back to eleventh in class/ fortieth overall to share Row 20 with Teddy Pilette's Dahm Argo Porsche. With only the bizarre Chevron recording less practice laps, the Tiga was proving good round the corners although relatively slow down that all-important three miles straightaway – top speed only around 290kph – as a result of the self-imposed, self-preserving rev limit. You could not help thinking, though, that another engine would have been more than welcome . . .

Saturday greeted everyone with incessant rain, continuing until lunch-time to leave the track still damp as Neil took that vital first stint although he was one of the very first to call in for more suitable tyres, the track already drying beneath his Avons.

As the race settled into its routine so Car 181 progressed, twenty-ninth overall after one hour, gaining a full eleven places by quarter distance. As Saturday night became Sunday morning the Abdex Tiga had climbed another three positions, completed one hundred laps and was now fourth in C2, chasing Charlie Ivey's Tiga turbo as Ecosse and the Spice Fiero went about their normal business ahead of the pack.

In the darkness of that still crowded pitlane team personnel looked as relaxed and optimistic as anyone could during such an event, their mysterious misfire a thing of the past. Neil Crang explained: "We are fifteenth overall, only a few laps off second in class," before continuing, "and have not really stopped for anything except tyres. We may change ratios and a gearbox rear end – it will take about twenty minutes – or may let sleeping dogs lie." They didn't, the long stop coming just before 4 a.m., the Metro V6 silent for half an hour, the transmission overhaul actuated as a precaution due to apparent question marks over Hewland FT internals being able to last a full twenty-four hours. This down time, referred to as a 12,000 miles service, also allowed vital minutes to check out the car

thoroughly as it braced itself for a long Sunday, twelve hours down and twelve to go. Rejoining, it had lost only four laps due to pace cars in the aftermath of Win Percy's horrific shunt, and one place, the GP/Cosmik Tiga DFL inheriting Dune's twelfth spot, a couple of hours to pass before the Abdex auto reasserted itself over the Metaxa machine.

By then it was daylight, dawn bringing positive if unspoken dreams of a good finish ever closer to reality, more now behind them than ahead, their battle not with Ivey, spice nor Ecosse but with themselves, the car and the place, *Le Circuit des 24 Heures* still ready to shatter their hopes at any show of weakness. The armco had its chance just then as 'DU' later explained: "The catch tank overflowed onto the right rear tyre. I felt it getting a bit funny at the back and as I turned in it must have sloshed some oil out and away I went, 360° through the

Porsche Curves without hitting a barrier! It went down the middle of the road, John Sheldon (Denim Tiga) came through the tyre smoke, I ended up facing the right way and carried on!" The fates had smiled kindly on Dune Motorsport.

Early morning fog still shrouded Mulsanne, only the mists of time separating all survivors of the night from a finish: it was 8 a.m., 'only' eight hours to go. The Abdex Tiga's reward for escaping the armco was to inherit tenth overall as Jaguar 6 was pushed away into retirement, this becoming ninth with third in C2 when Ivey's Porsche engine snapped the crankshaft two hours later, a portent of things to come. By now McNeil's team were changing brake discs as a matter of routine: trying, trying to eliminate any imponderable which may snatch defeat from the jaws of their own personal victory.

Six hours to go, five. The clock

ticked on, the laps went by, each passing of their car along the pits straight observed with tired eyes, everyone willing the Tiga ever onwards, as if the very act of watching its progress was a source of strength and inspiration to the machinery. Midday, four hours to go: seventeen laps behind Ecosse 102, seven laps clear of that Metaxa Tiga and Bassaler's charging Sauber. Three hours, it was looking good, the hard work surely done.

A routine pitstop and driver change just before 13H30 sent Jean Krucker on his way. He was soon back. Turning through Tertre Rouge onto Mulsanne something happened to the engine, the driver having no choice but to cruise pitwards, mobility reduced to a comparative crawl.

Off came the rear bodywork as eager hands went to work: searching and probing for a simple remedy, each and everyone hoping for a miracle. It was not to be. Although the Metro engine would run and could have made a 'Four O'Clock Special' damage was terminal, to be diagnosed as a broken crankshaft. The Dune Tiga was out, McNeil running a finger across his throat in age-old tradition to signify the end of a dream.

In those moments it was all over, the sole V6 failing to last the distance, those practice laps now proving crucial, their 260 race laps enough to make them highest non-finisher. It had been a brave effort, so near yet so far: a false dawn.

All were distraught, none hearing a tremendous round of sympathetic applause given by the crowd as Car 181 was pushed away, broken but unbowed. Everyone, with their own private sadness, looked to each other for solace, seeking the words, either silent or spoken, to express their disappointment.

"I am devastated" reiterated a weary Duncan Bain.

LEFT: After 260 laps, the car is out with a broken crankshaft.

TONY SOUTHGATE – DESIGNER GENES

Tony Southgate has been directly involved in top level motorsport design for over twenty five years, having started at Lola in January 1962. During the next 5½ years – including a brief sojourn at Brabham – he honed his skills on such famous machines as the Bowmaker V8 F.1., the Lola GT, forerunner of Ford's GT40 and the T130/Honda RE300 Grand Prix winner.

Then it was off to California with two years as Chief Designer to Dan Gurney's AAR 'Eagle' team, their GP project thwarted by funding, a subsequent 'Indycar' winning both the 1968 USAC title and The 500 itself, Dan the Man beaten into Victory Lane by Bobby Unser, another Eagle fourth. Gurney was second again in '69 while in both years a F5000 derivative took the national championship.

Returning to England in mid '69 Tony then produced the classic P153 then P160 for BRM, a last hurrah for the Bourne concern with great GP victories by Rodriguez/Spa '70, Siffert/Austria '71, Gethin/Monza '71 and Beltoise/Monaco '72 unable to stop the inevitable decline and fall of Louis Stanley's empire. His final BRM design, the P180 with novel wrap-around cockpit, scored a non-title race win but it was all too little too late . . .

Next came Shadow, a new project with big ideas which never really came to fruition. Tony conceived their first nine models including DN4 which won the 1974 CanAm trail. Of six GP types undeniably the best was DN5 yet unable to turn any of six 1975 pole positions into victory, their sole Grande Epreuve success destined to be with Alan Jones at Austria in 1977.

At that time Southgate was elsewhere, a fifteen month contract with Lotus endeavouring to put some gold into a JPS team's fortunes which had turned very black indeed, victory for Andretti in Japan their initial reward. It was a time when 'wing cars' and 'ground effects' became the buzz words of an era and things would never be quite the same again . . .

A brief spell back at Shadow then it was off to start Arrows, their initial *tipo* outlawed for copyright reasons, the consequential A1 never as competitive. This was replaced by the dramatic A2 which independently followed Chapman's Lotus 80 theory, both doomed as a design too far out yet a shape still appreciated by discerning people everywhere. This was superseded by the more conventional A3. Tony left Arrows in mid '80 for fresh challenges.

Since then freelance projects have included both early Theodores – the distinct high nose wing of TYO1 which was put to such good effect by Patrick Tambay. Tony's final GP car to date has been a 1983 Osella V12 which often embarrassed Alfa Romeo 'works' entries from whence the engines had come.

Whereas those cars exceeded expectations, both Ford projects were doomed by politics, the internal variety terminating a very promising Group C programme with a totally new chassis and Cosworth turbo engine – this becoming the basis of the Transit-styled 'Supervan' – and rule changes bringing the rally career of the RS200 to a premature halt. Although his original radical design had been 'productionised' to suit company philosophies it would have been interesting to observe the development of his first off-track competition car . . .

And now Jaguar. Should his XJRs ever win at the Sarthe his place in motorsport's history will be even more assured: the only designer to win Indianapolis, the Monaco GP and Le Mans. Quite an achievement for a Coventry lad who failed to secure an apprenticeship at his home town's most famous employer . . .

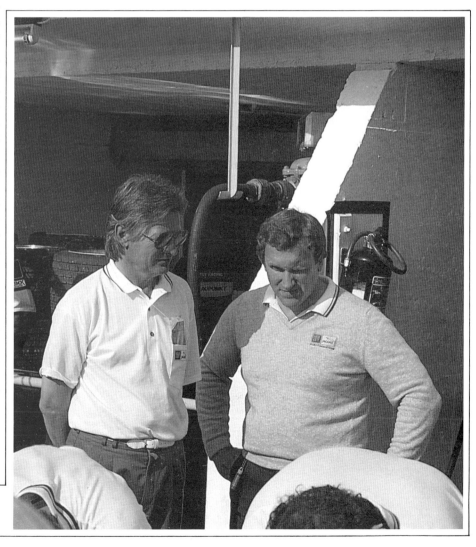

RIGHT: Tony Southgate (right) and Tom Walkinshaw ponder what the fates hold in store for them prior to the start of the race.

PURPLE PEN

In a village deep amidst the rolling acres of rural Northamptonshire there stands a large sandstone house, a warm and inviting place which functions not only as home for Tony Southgate but also his design studio. It is here his ideas for the Jaguar Group C sports racer were first committed to paper, here he strives to improve his creation, there I went to seek an insight into the design strategy and progress of this most significant project. While our meeting fell in that vital week between superb Silverstone victory and Le Mans Test Day, the story starts nearly three years earlier. And as with so many such ventures it commences with a telephone call:

"I got a 'phone call from Roger Silman of TWR who asked if I would be interested in a Group C car with a Jaguar V12 engine. He gave me some rough dimensions and weights and I thought 'Bloody Hell, you are going to be struggling there!' It is eighteen inches longer than a Cosworth V8, about 150 lbs heavier than a Porsche flat six with high centre of gravity besides being normally aspirated although I did appreciate – as a large capacity/slow revving unit – it would be theoretically more economical than either Porsche or Lancia. He put maximum emphasis on the chassis side of things, the only brief being to do

what I want, to go for Formula One type technology, all that modern stuff, and we agreed to do a deal."

Not a case of trying to cut a silk purse from a sow's ear, nevertheless it appeared the last thing a Jaguar racer apparently needed was a Jaguar engine, problems outweighing possibilities, this wondrous beastie superb for luxury limos such as an XJ12 or a Daimler Sovereign and excellent aboard a tin top racing XJS but as an out-and-out sports prototype at Silverstone, Monza, Le Mans . . . Somehow it all seemed a cameo of that hoary old joke whereby a stranger to the scene asks a local sage for directions only to be advised: "If I were you, I would not start from here!", Southgate having the same dilemma, his design to be dictated by a V12 with all those inherent competitive disadvantages, subsequent successes as much a tribute to his grey matter than its undoubted grunt.

Engine apart, it really was a case of carte blanche in all other aspects:

"I even went to Porsche for the gearbox – Jaguar weren't terribly excited about that of course! – who said they would sell us anything, very keen on brakes in a big way. Tom, Roger and I had a look around their factory where I was going to buy the gear cluster to put in our own casing but with Porsche its input shaft is high above the crown-

wheel and they drive down being a flat six, whereas in our layout it is low so you drive up. I thought of turning the crownwheel around the other side so they gave me drawings and bits but I subsequently dropped the idea having then discovered the March Indycar/ Sportscar 'box which I knew was better than a Hewland which had given trouble to Group 44. It works very well."

Mention of Bob Tullius' IMSA team who had done so much to revive Jaguar sporting interests not only with their Stateside activities but also Le Mans forays of 1984 and '85 raises an interesting aside regarding the TWR project and the ultimate fate of its famous four-valve-per-pot development first seen on that ill-fated XJ13 of two decades ago:

"Initially Jaguar had wanted Tom to race a modified Group 44 car over here so he said we would appraise it, yet the last thing he wanted to do was race someone else's car. Also his original approval was only to make a car, not to race it, subtle difference. Eventually we went to Snetterton with both, whizzing around and around, Martin Brundle driving. The Group 44 car went quite well although of course slower than our new one. It had a four-valve engine with about 700 bhp, far more than we had then. I did some calculations and although it was more powerful it was also a lot heavier so if you add that weight plus higher centre of gravity onto the normal two-valver around somewhere like Silverstone lap times come out the same; there was no advantage in using it. On that basis they scrapped the project . . . Another one of those swoops of the pen!"

All of this lay in the future as Tony set about drawing the shape of things to come. So where does one start?

"First of all, the design is totally dictated by the aerodynamic package,

LEFT: The design of the car is wholly dictated by the aerodynamic package, a Group C car being the most aerodynamically conscious of all by far, the entire surface being used. RIGHT: The chassis are made of Kevlar interwoven with carbon fibre and baked in TWR's own autoclave.

a Group C car being the most aerodynamically conscious of all by far, the whole surface being used. We do not have the restrictions of Formula One (open wheels etc.) who get most of their downforce from that massive rear wing which they drag along. They have got plenty of power and use it, the front wings really only to balance the car. It is crude and inefficient, relying on brute power whereas in Group C you have not got that much so you have to get drag down to a realistic level to get the fuel consumption. What I found quite difficult was arriving at the drag you can tolerate to establish a competitive lap time, but we got there and it has worked out okay ... It is a total aerodynamic package with the entire suspension layout arranged to suit that package. The front has horizontal dampers connected by a pushrod with very good wheel control while the rear goes inside the wheel as it is so big, only a vertical damper/spring in the airflow therefore allowing for big clean tunnels which make the back end very simple and light. I have fancied putting suspension within the wheels for ten years so it was quite pleasing to do so."

The chassis are made of Kevlar, interwoven with carbon fibre and baked in TWR's own autoclave, more 'modern stuff' used in such diverse items as rearwings, undertrays, doors and anti-roll bar, integrity of design and build subsequently to be dramatically proven by Win Percy a few weeks later. In a perverse way that accident

served to endorse Tony's comments about the structure, his praise unstinting when advising about incredible strength, a level of stiffness they found hard to measure and total lack of deterioration although Percy's 200 mph progress may not have helped the latter in that particular instance! The monocoque shape is highly significant to success although has not been without associate problems:

"Besides aerodynamics, the other essential is positioning of engine: being so big and heavy it is imperative to have it as far forward as possible, recessed into the rear bulkhead very close to the driver. Consequently it has a full width, small section fuel tank the shape of the seat with curved sections and lumps in it. There have been lots of problems with fuel collection systems, having about three goes at it. Originally there were three tanks with some behind the driver and some in the sills then last year it was all revised into one. This year the collector system is a lot better; at Silverstone the Watson/Lammers car finished with one litre in it.

"The first car came out quite well except being over engineered, needing a lot of weight pruning at something like 200 lbs over. So we nibbled away for '86 and it was pretty near the limit which made a big difference to performance. Then there were things like roll stiffness which we worked away at although that was quite hard to get right because the high centre of gravity makes it roll more than normal. This

year's XJR8 is quicker than expected as we have an engine improvement of about 40 bhp and are slightly more aerodynamically efficient with better wheel control on anti-roll bars. The whole thing has been cleaned up, all helping each other and instead of making what we expected to be a one second gain it has been two. The LM car is the same although on paper the figures are even better still. . . ."

A separate team-within-a-team has concentrated specifically on the task of Le Mans this year, such being the commitment by both Jaguar and TWR to win this classic event. Consequently three LM variants have evolved to concentrate on the rigours of a twenty four hours marathon and of Mulsanne, some amendments like a shorter and more convex nose section being subtle while a considerably shorter tail section is immediately obvious, especially without rear wheel spats.

"The car now has about 13% less drag and 25% more downforce than last year. It has taken a lot of work to achieve; detail studies, wind tunnels, testing etc. At Le Mans you have effectively got 79% of straightaways including Mulsanne so they dictate you must be quick there. Working back from the going rate which last year was about 220 mph, you arrive at a drag factor you have got to achieve then try to produce as much downforce as possible to still do that speed. You need a different aerodynamic package of tunnels, wings, tails etc. We actually did 221 which was very pleasing as we had come under a lot of pressure from people who said we couldn't achieve it. I put a lot of effort into that – it was quite worrying! A weak area last year was the driveline but now the engine is at an angle ($2\frac{1}{2}°$ upwards towards the rear) to straighten it out and we have put in bigger constant driveshafts and velocity joints – the same size as used by Porsche – to eliminate any such problems. The penalty is a higher centre of gravity, however at Le Mans the emphasis is not on road holding; if you lose half a second a lap by angling the engine so what? Because at the end of the race, if the joints haven't seized up you are still in it!

"This year there is a big hole at the back, a big gap between tail and tunnel to get the air out thereby improving underbonnet temperatures – last year the starter motor tried to melt on Derek Warwick's car – plus extra louvres and big scoops. Of course there are more and better lights while items such as wishbones, axles and wheels remain unchanged, brake discs thicker to avoid cracking. The bodywork is 50% thicker too, and more practical. Last year it all stuck out at the back, far too vulnerable. In retrospect we did not really have much idea, just turned up for the Test Day, were quickest and thought 'This is easy'. Then went back for the race. . . ."

They have come a long way since then, the Jaguars now able to offer a very positive and consistent challenge to Porsche domination, four consecutive wins the ideal fillip for Sarthe success yet by the very virtue of their own separate Le Mans venture, all knowing the next sequential number is not necessarily five. But win or lose no doubt they would all learn:

"You are never satisfied with a car. There is always something. . . ."

1. Four larger and more powerful headlamps replaced the normal two units in a reprofiled nose. 2. A broader and lower rear wing was mounted further back than usual.

Three Silk Cut sponsored XJR8-LMs were taken to La Sarthe, two being conversions from 1986 monocoques with the third a new tub, this being chassis -387/Car 4 which visually differed from its predecessors by dint of a horizontally split chassis panel beneath the doors for easier access/repair and a single NACA roof duct, both older cars having twin vents.

The newest XJR first ran a few days after Silverstone where -186/Car 6 had appeared in Le Mans trim for Brundle/Neilsen, the trio completed by -286/3 Car 5 in which Messrs Cheever and Warwick won the 1000 kms twelve months before. Other identifying marks concerned colour coded Jaguar 'sun visors' and roof lights: 4 – white and yellow, 5 – orange and green, 6 – yellow and white respectively.

Although they produced substantially more downforce than last time, the three LMs had about one-third less than in sprint form, that term applying to all other events, be they 360 kms or Six Hours. Four larger and more powerful headlamps replaced the normal two units in a re-profiled nose while the short-tail, sans wheelspats, was complemented by a broader and lower wing mounted further back than usual.

The angled engine – something first tried by Southgate with his Arrows A2 back in 1979 – was exactly as specified for all other events, drivers restricted to about 400 rpm less than elsewhere.

They weighed in at about 875/800 kgs whereas normally the high spec cars are required to carry low spec lead ballast to reach the category's minimum limit, most of this excess due to thicker bodywork to ward off flak damage during Les Vingt Quatre Heures du Mans.

FIRST OF THE MANY

Building twenty five cars to a new specification before one had turned a wheel in anger is not the accepted method of developing an endurance racing machine, yet such was the modus operandi used by Porsche to produce the model which brought their first outright victory at Le Mans, the 917.

The reasons for this inadvisable multiple birth were, perhaps not surprisingly, circumvention of rules for it had been decreed by the CSI that from 1968 there would be Sports Prototypes limited to three litres and Production Sportscars of up to 5000 cc, the latter requiring a minimum of fifty built examples to qualify. This became twenty-five a year later, the official objective of getting away from those seven litre/200 mph monsters of Ford or Chaparral on grounds of safety superseded by more earthly requirements to stimulate competition levels. It would do so enormously although not in any way ever envisaged by the authorities, nobody having considered it possible that entrants might build such numbers of what were, in effect, Production Prototypes, their thoroughbred racing engines far beyond stockblock based Detroit Iron.

Stuttgart's design brief required introducing as few unknown factors as possible, much being directly related to the 908 they were already successfully campaigning; a tubular space-frame chassis very similar in concept although aluminium replaced steel while the power unit borrowed items such as pistons, conrods and valves from its older sister as a three litre flat eight effectively became the basis from which grew a 4.5 litre twelve cylinder.

Although this all saved very valuable development time it did not make the 917 the immediate success of its predecessor, indeed it was nigh on a calamity! Debuting at Spa Francorchamps in May '69, Jo Siffert and Brian Redman claimed pole position then promptly showed their relief at reverting to a 908 by winning the race while Mitter and Schutz were nowhere men in their 'other' 917. From the Ardennes it was onto the arduous 'Ring with Frank Gardner and David Piper drafted in when Hahne and Quester withdrew, discretion transcending Teutonic valour, eighth their reward for a brave effort in an unwieldy machine.

All these problems, with experienced drivers actually refusing to race the beast, related not to speed but handling – more precisely the lack of it! – these fearsomely fast projectiles very unstable and virtually uncontrollable, soon to prove lethal, Gardner suggesting that if a driver 'lost it' he would need a compass to refind the track . . .

Despite such reservations three examples appeared at Le Mans, their headaches compounded when the movable rear spoilers were banned, Porsche thus threatening to withdraw *all* their cars from the event. With Rolf Stommelen/Kurt Ahrens on pole position and another 917 alongside followed by a brace of 908s this would have decimated the grid so hastily a 'compromise' was reached: Porsche had ailerons, Le Mans their race . . .

Sadly it did not alleviate all Porsche's troubles, John Woolfe fatally crashing his private short-tailed 917 in flames at White House on lap one as both 'works' cars led, the pole position machine retaining its advantage for an hour before falling back then out with oil pressure and clutch problems, retiring before dawn. A 908 took over for Siffert and Redman, only to disappear with gearbox difficulties two hours later, the resolute 917 of Vic Elford/Richard Attwood now clear of the rest, a bevy of not-so-beautiful 908s cushioning it from outsiders, Matra sixth with the Gulf GT40s next, taking advantage of others' misfortunes, as darkness fell over la Sarthe.

When the sun rose again on a beautiful morning, this pair of orange and blue Fords were third and fourth, mirroring what would become a fine day for John Wyer's team as they chased the Porsches, Elford/Attwood now six laps ahead of a 908 for Lins/Kauhsen with Hermann/Larrousse fifth and headed for a dramatic showdown. Onward they went, time ticking away when, with only 3½ hours to go, the second placed car broke, soon to be followed by its leader, both succumbing to that Porsche bête-noire of transmission faults. Within thirty minutes defeat had been snatched from the clutches of victory and despite a magnificently valiant attempt by Hans Hermann he was not able to resist Jacky Ickx (and Jackie Oliver) taking chassis 1075 to a second consecutive victory, an official margin of 120 metres seeming even closer in photographs . . .

Porsche were mortified; they had won the Makes title via their 908s yet failed to take its biggest prize, the only course seemingly open being: if you cannot beat 'em, join 'em. Indeed team manager Rico Steinemann had approached John Wyer in March to discuss an unprecedented offer about JW Automotive running the Porsche factory team in 1970/71 so these two Le Mans defeats at his hands must have had bitter-sweet connotations *chez* Porsche.

Arrangements agreed, JWA were invited to a test session at the Österreichring in October, this newly opened track having witnessed a one–

111

three success by 917s two months after Le Mans, a delayed Siffert/Ahrens winning a race of attrition by over a minute, handling improved although still far from good. The programme was to finalise specifications for next year, the test car fitted with a short 'kurz' tail as opposed to their alternative long 'langheck' version but despite suspension changes no significant improvement in the temperament of either car or drivers resulted, a basic aerodynamic fault being suspected. What to do?

Also present was a Can-AM type barchetta with its even shorter/higher tail and to the undoubted, if unspoken, horror of Porsche people men from JWA set about cannibalising it to fit the coupé by virtue of cutters, sheet aluminium and self tapping screws. The muletta immediately proved more stable – and three seconds a lap quicker . . .

More development soon followed and would be imperative as Ferrari had now also built the necessary twenty-five examples of their 512S when racing got under way again at Daytona in January, Porsche responding to this threat by increasing engine capacity to 4.9 litres, the first car so equipped debuting at Monza. It became a battle of giants, both marques having customers to back up 'factory' teams, Germany bettering Italy on most accounts as they all prepared for Le Mans, JW Automotive definitely the team to beat with five victories so far plus their superb Le Mans record of recent seasons.

There were no less than fifty one cars lined up striving for honours including a quartet of Alfas and three Matras yet most people considered there to be only one truly significant duel for victory as eleven of Maranello's finest were pitted against seven 917s. Two were langhecks, the remainder short-tails including all three JWA cars, Wyer and team manager David Yorke unwilling to trade any benefit of extra speed down Mulsanne for inferior handling elsewhere. Anyway, longtails were bound to be more fatiguing should it rain . . .

Ironically, although unsurprisingly, an extended version qualified on pole position, Elford/Ahrens taking their Porsche Salzburg flyer around two-tenths quicker than Vaccarella/Giunti's 512S, the next couple of rows a colourful mixture of orange and blue with Italian scarlet, the top fourteen places equally shared by both manufacturers. It had all the makings of an epic battle, one flagged off by no less a personage than Doctor Ferry Porsche himself. Would his presence waive the curse, could Porsche finally win Le Mans?

They took an early lead, Elford duelling with Siffert throughout that first hour with fellow JWA teamsters Pedro Rodriguez and David Hobbs next up although both would be out by suppertime, the Mexican when his cooling fan broke, Hobbs/Hailwood after 'Mike the Bike' hit a stranded Alfa at Dunlop Curve. By then Ferrari had lost *five* cars, their fastest qualifier lasting only a few laps before its engine broke while four more were eliminated almost as one, Wisell's slow moving 512S struck by Regazzoni who was, in turn, hit by Mike Parkes in another notorious White House contretemps, debutant Derek Bell narrowly surviving all this mayhem unscathed only for his engine to immediately expire. It was destruction derby time, the race less than four hours old, rain now falling quite heavily . . .

Now all Ferrari's main hopes lay with Ickx/Peter Schetty, their 512S sixth behind five remaining 917s but into third within a couple of hours then second at midnight as a puncture slowed Elford/Ahrens, the rain abating awhile. They were carrying the fight to Porsche, 'Seppi' and Redman four laps ahead, the Belgian having proved last year his ability of pacing a finish – and there were still sixteen hours to go, anything could happen.

Alas, when it did the results were tragic, this fine encounter ending when the leaders arrived at Ford Chicane together shortly before two o'clock, Ickx locking a brake, spinning off and killing a marshall. The Scuderia's challenge effectively ended there and then.

A few minutes later the race was all over for JWA, their hopes of a Sarthe hat-trick shattered by a broken engine, Siffert stating it had over-revved after jumping out of gear thereby leaving Richard Attwood/Hans Hermann ahead. Almost unnoticed in all this drama the private AAW Porsche of Gijs van Lennep/David Piper, having been third briefly on Saturday evening before a nose damaging/time consuming spin, crashed out on Mulsanne when a tyre exploded at speed.

Willi Kauhsen/Gerard Larrousse were now second, their psychedelic Martini cocktail langheck two laps adrift, a bid for glory thwarted when rain returned around half time, drowning electrics, allowing Elford/Ahrens back ahead, a Porsche Salzburg one-two, short leading long. Another Martini car, the Porsche 908 of Rudi Lins/Helmut Marko inherited third, this becoming second at breakfast time when the pole position car, so long a front runner and possible victor, choked on an inlet valve.

Throughout the morning interest concentrated as to whether a Martini 917LH could catch a Martini 908, finally achieving it when sunshine briefly reappeared around noon, this being the final significant act of a sodden and, often, anticlimatic event. Reeling off those last few hours the winning pair avenged their immense disappointments from '69, proving the adage that to finish first – first you have to finish. In fact, in qualifying the winners had been slowest 917, Kauhsen/Larrousse, now five laps adrift, next so. Both cars were fitted with the 'older' 4.5 litre units. Only seven cars were classified as finishers, all Porsches bar two lone surviving 512Ss in fourth and fifth, well beaten even by that open topped three litre. Stuttgart claimed all three class categories, Indexes of Performance and Thermal Efficiency with fastest lap credited to Vic Elford as per last year. They had not beaten the opposition but crushed them and, despite the circumstances, with some style.

On their twentieth visit to Le Mans Porsche had finally scored outright victory. Their tally now stands at a dozen, the latest exactly seventeen years to the day since their first. It must be easy when you know how . . .

PRACTICE TIMES

	No.	Drivers	Marques	GR	Session 1	Session 2	Time	Session	Speed	Laps
1.	18	Porsche AG Mass, Wollek, Schuppan	Porsche 962 C	C1	3'21.09	3'33.33	3'21.09	1	242.309	55
2.	17	Porsche AG Stuck, Bell, Holbert	Porsche 962 C	C1	3'21.13	3'27.29	3'21.13	1	242.261	61
3.	4	Silk Cut Jaguar Cheever, Boesel	Jaguar XJR-8	C1	3'30.43	3'24.36	3'24.36	2	238.432	52
4.	6	Silk Cut Jaguar Nielsen, Brundle, Hahne	Jaguar XJR-8	C1	3'29.63	3'24.68	3'24.68	2	238.859	53
5.	5	Silk Cut Jaguar Watson, Lammers, Percy	Jaguar XJR-8	C1	3'27.56	3'24.90	3'24.90	2	237.803	57
6.	13	Primagaz Competition Courage, Raphanel, Regout	Cougar Porsche	C1	3'29.03	3'26.21	3'26.21	2	236.293	64
7.	62	Kouros Racing Ganassi, Dumfries, Thackwell	Kouros Mercedes	C1	3'26.58	3'41.36	3'26.58	1	235.869	68
8.	61	Kouros Racing Pescarolo, Thackwell, Okada	Kouros Mercedes	C1	3'29.76	3'27.41	3'27.41	2	234.925	46
9.	7	Joest Racing Van der Merwe, Robinson, Haywood	Porsche 962 C	C1	3'27.53	3'34.78	3'27.53	1	234.790	34
10.	15	Equipe Liqui Moly Cobb, Palmer, Weaver	Porsche 962 C	C1	3'31.49	3'30.22	3'30.22	2	231.785	48
11.	8	Joest Racing Dickens, Jelinski, Hobbs	Porsche 962 C	C1	3'31.38	3'37.87	3'31.38	1	230.513	55
12.	2	Brun Motorsport Larrauri, Schafer, Pareja	Porsche 962 C	C1	3'32.98	3'41.24	3'32.98	1	228.782	34
13.	51	Secateva Pessiot, Raulet, Migault	WM P 86	C1	3'33.92	3'44.94	3'33.92	1	227.776	54
14.	36	Toyota Team Tom's Jones, Lees, Elgh	Toyota 87 C	C1	3'39.18	3'34.45	3'34.45	2	227.213	61
15.	11	Porsche Kremer Racing Fouche, Konrad, Taylor	Porsche 962 C	C1	3'38.04	3'34.50	3'34.50	2	227.160	55
16.	37	Toyota Team Tom's Sekiya, Hoshino, Needell	Toyota 87 C	C1	3'39.69	3'34.89	3'34.89	2	226.748	74
17.	23	Nissan Motorsports Hoshino, Takahashi, Matsumoto	Nissan R 87 E	C1	3'35.99	4'26.05	3'35.99	1	225.593	49
18.	72	Primagaz Competition Yver, De Dryver, Lassig	Porsche 962 C	C1	3'41.34	3'36.76	3'36.76	2	224.792	58
19.	10	Porsche Kremer Racing Nissen, Weidler, Takahashi	Porsche 962 C	C1	3'37.46	3'45.90	3'37.46	1	224.068	47
20.	32	Nissan Motorsports Hasemi, Wada, Suzuki	Nissan R 87 E	C1	3'38.13	3'47.34	3'38.13	1	223.380	40
21.	52	Secateva Dorchy, Gache, Delestre	WM P 87	C1	3'50.96	3'38.68	3'38.68	2	222.818	48
22.	127	Chamberlain Engineering Adams, Jones, Duxbury	Spice Pontiac Fiero	C2	3'54.66	3'40.02	3'40.02	2	221.461	34
23.	3	Brun Motorsport Spenard, Adam, Goodyear	Porsche 962 C	C1	3'56.11	3'40.71	3'40.71	2	220.769	53

PRACTICE TIMES

	No.	Drivers	Marques		Hours	Laps	Kms		Average	Group
24.	29	Italya Sports Olofsson, Ferte, Gonin	Nissan R 86 V	C1	3'41.46	4'10.55	3'41.46	1	220.021	46
25.	111	Spice Engineering Ltd. Spice, De Henning, Velez	Spice Pontiac Fiero	C2	3'42.28	3'54.03	3'42.28	1	219.210	48
26.	1	Brun Motorsport Belmondo, Trolle, De Thoisy	Porsche 962 C	C1	3'53.29	3'44.31	3'44.31	2	217.226	42
27.	201	Mazda Speed Co. Ltd. Terada, Katayama, Yorino	Mazda 757	IM	3'45.56	3'49.83	3'45.56	1	216.022	53
28.	202	Mazda Speed Co. Ltd. Kennedy, Dieudonne, Galvin	Mazda 757	IM	3'49.35	3'47.53	3'47.53	2	214.151	58
29.	42	Noel Dell Bello Lombardi, Guillot, Lempereur	Sauber C8	C1	3'48.44	3'48.16	3'48.16	2	213.560	68
30.	123	Charles Ivey Racing Cohen Olivar, Cooper, Dodd-Noble	T16A 6C 287	C2	3'50.33	3'59.89	3'50.33	1	211.548	39
31.	203	Porsche AG Metge, Haldi, Nierop	Porsche 961	IM	3'50.86	3'55.46	3'50.86	1	211.062	49
32.	40	Graff Racing Terrien, Rahier, Grand	Rondeau 482	C1	4'11.61	3'52.90	3'52.90	2	209.214	48
33.	102	Swiftair/Ecurie Ecosse Mallock, Duez, Leslie	Ecosse C 286	C2	4'37.81	3'53.37	3'53.37	2	208.792	42
34.	125	Patrick Oudet Sotty, Justice, Oudet	Tiga GC 85	C2	4'11.64	3'56.62	3'56.62	2	205.925	29
35.	101	Swiftair/Ecurie Ecosse Wilds, Petery, Delano	Ecosse C 286	C2	3'57.06	4'07.86	3'57.06	1	205.542	58
36.	117	Lucky Strike Schance Hoy, Smith, Schanche	Argo JM 19	C2	3'57.21	4'07.23	3'57.21	1	205.412	50
37.	116	Luigi Taverna Taverna, Clements, Trucco	Alba AR3	C2	4'04.47	3'58.39	3'58.39	2	204.396	38
38.	177	Louis Descartes Descartes, Heuclin, Lacaud	ALD 03	C2	4'00.85	4'00.07	4'00.07	2	202.965	42
39.	200	Dahm Cars Racing Fritsch, Pilette, Libert	Argo JM 19	C2	4'06.92	4'01.40	4'01.40	2	201.847	57
40.	181	Dune Motorsport Krucker, Crang, Bain	Tiga GC 287	C2	4'03.00	4'07.57	4'03.00	1	200.518	27
41.	198	RBR Andrews, Peters, Allison	Tiga GC 286	C2	4'12.49	4'03.40	4'03.40	2	200.188	44
42.	121	Cosmick/G.P. Motorsport Los, Wood, Hessert	Tiga GC 287	C2	4'03.79	4'03.77	4'03.77	2	199.885	47
43.	114	Tiga Ford DK Thyrring, Sheldon, Harrower	Tiga GC 287	C2	4'11.73	4'03.85	4'83.85	2	199.819	38
44.	178	Louis Descartes Tremblay, Lateste, Boulay	ALD 02	C2	4'07.21	4'04.02	4'04.02	2	199.680	44
45.	108	Roland Bassaler Yvon, Hervalet, Bourjade	Sauber S.H.S.C6	C2	4'06.55	4'11.59	4'06.55	1	197.631	48
46.	103	Barlett Racing Goodman Boutinaud, Donovan, Lee Davey	Bardon DB2	C2	4'17.41	4'06.83	4'06.83	2	197.407	41
47.	118	Olindo Jacobelli Iacobelli, Ricci, Tessier	Royale RP40	C2	4'06.88	4'08.81	4'06.88	1	197.367	30
48.	113	Jose Thibault Thibault, Heinrich	Chevron	C2	4'14.30	4'43.20	4'14.30	1	191.608	22

AT 10.00 pm SATURDAY

	No.	Drivers	Marques	Hours	Laps	Kms	Average	Group
1.	6	Brundle, Nielsen, Hahne	Jaguar XJR-8	5h57'16.2	95	1286	215.941	C1
2.	5	Lammers, Watson, Percy	Jaguar XJR-8	5H57'17.0	94	1272	213,660	C1
3.	17	Stuck, Bell, Holbert	Porsche 962 C	5h57'43.8	94	1272	213.393	C1
4.	15	Palmer, Weaver, Cobb	Porsche 962 C	5h57'03.1	93	1259	211.524	C1
5.	4	Cheever, Boesel	Jaguar XJR-8	5h59'25.6	93	1259	210.127	C1
6.	72	Lassig, Yver, De Dryver	Porsche 962 C	5h57'13.9	89	1205	202.325	C1
7.	292	Kennedy, Galvin, Dieudonne	Mazda 757	5h57'59.0	87	1178	197.363	IM
8.	13	Raphanel, Courage, Regout	Cougar Porsche	5h59'06.9	86	1164	194.479	C1
9.	102	Leslie, Mallock, Duez	Ecosse C 286	5h57'28.8	85	1150	193.097	C2
10.	203	Metge, Haldi, Nierop	Porsche 961	5h58'27.2	85	1150	192.573	IM
11.	29	Olofsson, Ferte, Gonin	Nissan R86V	5h59'03.5	85	1150	192.248	C1
12.	11	Fouche, Konrad, Taylor	Porsche 962 C	5h57'11.9	84	1137	190.976	C1
13.	3	Adam, Spenard, Goodyear	Porsche 962 C	5h57'45.7	84	1137	190.675	C1
14.	123	Cooper, Dodd-Noble, Cohen-Olivar	Tiga GC 287	5h58'47.1	83	1123	187.868	C2
15.	111	Spice, Velez, De Henning	Spice Pontiac Fiero	5h59'55.9	83	1123	187.269	C2
16.	23	Hoshino, Takahashi, Matsumoto	Nissan R87E	5h58'17.3	82	1110	185.862	C1
17.	1	Trolle, Belmondo, De Thoisy	Porsche 962 C	5h56'38.7	81	1096	184.441	C1
18.	181	Crang, Krucker, Bain	Tiga GC 287	5h57'18.7	78	1056	177.278	C2
19.	177	Heuclin, Lacaud, Descartes	ALD 03	5h51'54.1	77	1042	177.696	C2
20.	121	Wood, Los, Hessert	Tiga GC 287	5h56'30.5	77	1042	175.400	C2
21.	101	Wilds, Delano, Petery	Ecosse C 286	5h57'38.0	76	1029	172.577	C2
22.	198	Allison, Andrews, Peters	Tiga GC 286	5h53'12.9	75	1015	172.437	C2
23.	125	Justice, Oudet, Sotty	Tiga GC 85	5h57'53.9	75	1015	170.181	C2
24.	40	Grand, Rahier, Terrien	Rondeau 482	5h51'40.5	71	961	163.955	C1
25.	178	Lateste, Tremblay, Boulay	Ald 02	5h50'59.2	69	934	159.649	C2
26.	103	Lee Davey, Donovan, Boutinaud	Bardon DB2	5h53'27.2	68	920	156.237	C2
27.	116	Taverna, Clements, Trucco	Alba AR3	5h55'08.5	68	920	155.495	C2
28.	108	Yvon, Hervalet, Guillot	Sauber S.H.S.C6	5h56'46.8	65	880	147.952	C2
29.	114	Thyrring, Sheldon, Harrower	Tiga GC 287	5h55'46.0	63	853	143.808	C2
30.	61	Thackwell, Pescarolo, Okada	Kouros Mercedes	5h45'39.8	61	826	143.313	C1
31.	127	Adams, Duxbury, Jones	Spice Pontiac Fiero	5h57'43.4	60	812	136.211	C2
32.	32	Hasemi, Wada, Suzuki	Nissan R87E	5h57'32.8	59	799	134.007	C1
		Best lap						
	62	Dumfries, Ganassi, Thackwell	Kouros Mercedes	3'25.4	24		237.224	
		Retired						
	7	Van der Merve, Hobbs, Robinson	Porsche 962 C	0h19'04.8	4	54		
	42	Lombardi, Lempereur, Cuynet	Sauber C8	0h18'42.2	4	54		
	117	Schanche, Hoy, Smith	Argo JM 19	0h24'42.7	5	68		
	10	Nissen, Weidler, Takahashi	Porsche 962 C	0h25'48.7	6	81		
	8	Jelinski, Dickens, Haywood	Porsche 962 C	0h29'35.3	7	95		
	200	Fritsch, Pilette, Libert	Argo JM 19	0h54'58.8	12	162		
	118	Iacobelli, Ricci, Tessier	Royale RP40	3h54'32.4	13	176		
	52	Dorchy, Gache, Delestre	WM P 87	3h16'58.3	13	176		
	51	Raulet, Migault, Pessiot	WM P 86	1h02'20.4	14	189		
	18	Wollek, Mass, Schuppan	Porsche 962 C	1h00'49.1	16	217		
	113	Thibault, Heinrich	Chevron	2h48'41.8	18	244		
	36	Jones, Lees, Elgh	Toyota 87 C	1h15'42.4	19	257		
	201	Katayama, Terada, Yorino	Mazda 757	2h35'53.2	34	460		
	62	Dumfries, Ganassi, Thackwell	Kouros Mercedes	2h26'53.8	37	501		
	37	Needell, Sekiya, Hoshino	Toyota 87 C	4h27'23.5	39	528		
	2	Larrauri, Pareja, Schafer	Porsche 962 C	2h37'24.6	40	541		

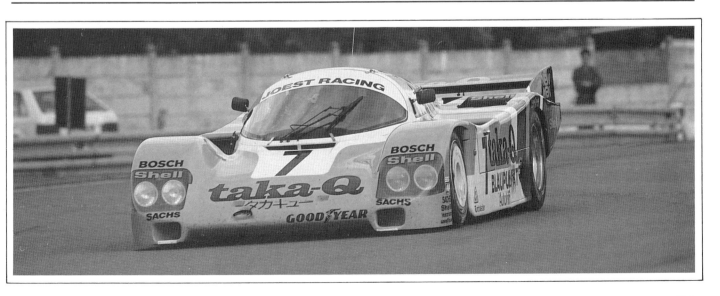

AT 4.00 am SUNDAY

	No.	Drivers	Marques	Hours	Laps	Kms	Average	Group
1.	17	Stuck, Bell, Holbert	Porsche 962 C	11h56'12.0	174	2355	197.298	C1
2.	6	Brundle, Nielsen, Hahne	Jaguar XJR-8	11h53'42.9	173	2342	196.847	C1
3.	4	Cheever, Boesel	Jaguar XJR-8	11h53'48.0	172	2328	195.686	C1
4.	72	Lassig, Yver, De Dryver	Porsche 962 C	11h56'13.7	162	2193	183.684	C1
5.	13	Raphanel, Courage, Regout	Cougar Porsche	11h53'47.1	161	2179	183.175	C1
6.	11	Fouche, Konrad, Taylor	Porsche 962 C	11h53'45.9	159	2152	180.905	C1
7.	102	Leslie, Mallock, Duez	Ecosse C 286	11h53'40.0	156	2111	177.516	C2
8.	23	Hoshino, Takahashi, Matsumoto	Nissan R87E	11h57'32.2	151	2044	170.935	C1
9.	202	Kennedy, Galvin, Dieudonne	Mazda 757	11h53'41.2	150	2030	170.684	IM
10.	111	Spice, Velez, De Henning	Spice Pontiac Fiero	11h56'16.2	150	2030	170.068	C2
11.	123	Cooper, Dodd-Noble, Cohen-Olivar	Tiga GC 287	11h53'44.5	149	2017	169.533	C2
12.	181	Crang, Krucker, Bain	Tiga GC 287	11h49'46.0	145	1963	165.905	C2
13.	121	Wood, Los, Hessert	Tiga GC 287	11h57'21.9	145	1963	164.148	C2
14.	203	Metge, Haldi, Nierop	Porsche 961	11h56'18.7	139	1881	157.587	IM
15.	40	Grand, Rahier, Terrien	Rondeau 482	11h57'19.7	138	1868	156.232	C1
16.	125	Justice, Oudet, Sotty	Tiga GC 85	11h53'51.1	136	1841	154.717	C2
17.	101	Wilds, Delano, Petery	Ecosse C 286	11h06'20.0	135	1827	164.532	C2
18.	198	Allison, Andrews, Peters	Tiga GC 286	11h53'54.6	130	1760	147.879	C2
19.	108	Yvon, Hervalet, Guillot	Sauber S.H.S.C6	11h59'23.3	128	1732	144.496	C2
20.	116	Taverna, Clements, Trucco	Alba AR3	11h06'41.4	126	1705	153.481	C2
21.	103	Lee Davey, Donovan, Boutinaud	Bardon DB2	11h56'20.2	126	1705	142.844	C2
22.	177	Heuclin, Lacaud, Descartes	Ald 03	11h57'24.6	124	1678	140.366	C2
23.	114	Thyrring, Sheldon, Harrower	Tiga GC 287	11h57'22.5	122	1651	138.109	C2
24.	61	Thackwell, Pescarolo, Okada	Kouros Mercedes	11h53'50.4	118	1597	134.242	C1
25.	178	Lateste, Tremblay, Boulay	ALD 02	11h56'17.6	118	1597	133.782	C2
26.	32	Hasemi, Wada, Suzuki	Nissan R87E	11h56'15.2	104	1408	117.916	C1
27.	127	Adams, Duxbury, Jones	Spice Pontiac Fiero	10h36'13.1	86	1164	109.774	C2
		Best lap						
	62	Dumfries, Ganassi, Thackwell	Kouros Mercedes	3'25.4	24		237.224	
		Retired						
	7	Van Der Merve, Hobbs, Robinson	Porsche 962 C	0h19'04.8	4	54		
	42	Lombardi, Lempereur, Cuynet	Sauber C8	0h18'42.2	4	54		
	117	Schanche, Hoy, Smith	Argo JM 19	0h24'42.7	5	68		
	10	Nissen, Weidler, Takahashi	Porsche 962 C	0h25'48.7	6	81		
	8	Jellinski, Dickens, Haywood	Porsche 962 C	0h29'35.3	7	95		
	200	Fritsch, Pilette, Libert	Argo JM 19	0h54'58.8	12	162		
	118	Iacobelli, Ricci, Tessier	Royal RP40	3h54'32.4	13	176		
	52	Dorchy, Gache, Delestre	WM P 87	3h16'58.3	13	176		
	51	Raulet, Migault, Pessiot	WM P 86	1h01'20.4	14	189		
	18	Wollek, Mass, Schuppan	Porsche 962 C	1h00'49.1	16	217		
	113	Thibault, Heinrich	Chevron	2h48'41.8	18	244		
	36	Jones, Lees, Elgh	Toyota 87 C	1h15'42.4	19	257		
	201	Katayama, Terada, Yorino	Mazda 757	2h39'53.2	34	460		
	62	Dumfries, Ganassi, Thackwell	Kouros Mercedes	2h26'53.8	37	501		
	37	Needell, Sekiya, Hoshino	Toyota 87 C	4h27'23.5	39	528		
	2	Larrauri, Pareja, Schafer	Porsche 962 C	2h37'24.6	40	541		
	29	Olofsson, Ferte, Gonin	Nissan R 86 V	6h06'35.4	86	1164		
	1	Trolle, Belmondo, De Thoisy	Porsche 962 C	6h33'05.4	88	1191		
	15	Palmer, Weaver, Cobb	Porsche 962 C	7h23'47.6	112	1516		
	3	Adam, Spenard, Goodyear	Porsche 962 C	8h54'48.2	120	1624		
	5	Lammers, Watson, Percy	Jaguar XJR-8	10h40'01.5	158	2139		

AT 10.00 am SUNDAY

	No.	Drivers	Marques	Hours	Laps	Kms	Average	Group
1.	17	Stuck, Bell, Holbert	Porsche 962 C	17h54'45.9	261	3533	197.213	C1
2.	4	Cheever, Boesel	Jaguar XJR-8	17h54'40.5	245	3316	185.139	C1
3.	72	Lassig, Yver, De Dryver	Porsche 962 C	17h54'42.4	245	3316	185.133	C1
4.	13	Raphanel, Courage, Regout	Cougar Porshce	17h57'31.6	242	3275	182.388	C1
5.	11	Fouche, Konrad, Taylor	Porsche 962 C	17h57'30.4	240	3248	180.884	C1
6.	111	Spice, Velez, De Henning	Spice Pontiac Fiero	17h57'36.8	232	3140	174.837	C2
7.	102	Leslie, Mallock, Duez	Ecosse C 286	17H54'44.3	230	3113	173.793	C2
8.	202	Kennedy, Galvin, Dieudonne	Mazda 757	17h54'45.3	229	3100	173.035	IM
9.	123	Cooper, Dodd-Noble, Cohen-Olivar	Tiga GC 287	17h55'49.0	223	3018	168.335	C2
10.	181	Crang, Krucker, Bain	Tiga GC 287	17h57'28.0	216	2924	162.801	C2
11.	121	Wood, Los, Hessert	Tiga GC 287	17h54'46.4	207	2802	156.409	C2
12.	40	Grand, Rahier, Terrien	Rondeau 482	17h32'05.8	201	2721	155.149	C1
13.	108	Yvon, Hervalet, Guillot	Sauber S.H.S.C6	17h51'19.7	198	2680	150.090	C2
14.	177	Heuclin, Lacaud, Descartes	ALD 03	17h57'36.5	194	2626	146.200	C2
15.	114	Thyrring, Sheldon, Harrower	Tiga GC 287	17h57'37.4	194	2626	146.198	C2
16.	103	Lee Davey, Donovan, Boutinaud	Bardon DB2	15h59'21.2	172	2328	145.599	C2
17.	116	Taverna, Clements, Trucco	Alba AR3	17h55'52.5	172	2328	129.830	C2
18.	178	Lateste, Tremblay, Boulay	ALD 02	17h57'38.3	161	2179	121.328	C2
19.	172	Adams, Duxbury, Jones	Spice Pontiac Fiero	17h55'53.4	157	2125	118.506	C2

	Best lap							
	62	Dumfries, Ganassi, Thackwell	Kouros Mercedes	3'25.4	24		237.224	

	Retired							
	7	Van Der Merve, Hobbs, Robinson	Porsche 962 C	0h19'04.8	4	54		
	42	Lombardi, Lempereur, Cuynet	Sauber C8	0h18'42.2	4	54		
	117	Schanche, Hoy, Smith	Argo JM 19	0h24'42.7	5	68		
	10	Nissen, Weidler, Takahashi	Porsche 962 C	0h25'48.7	6	81		
	8	Jelinski, Dickens, Haywood	Porsche 962 C	0h29'35.3	7	95		
	200	Fritsch, Pilette, Libert	Argo JM 19	0h54'58.8	12	162		
	118	Iacobelli, Ricci, Tessier	Royal RP40	3h54'32.4	13	176		
	52	Dorchy, Gache, Delestre	WM P 87	3h16'58.3	13	176		
	51	Raulet, Migault, Pessiot	WM P 86	1h01'20.4	14	189		
	18	Wollek, Mass, Schuppan	Porsche 962 C	1h00'49.1	16	217		
	113	Thibault, Heinrich	Chevron	2h48'41.8	18	244		
	36	Jones, Lees, Elgh	Toyota 87 C	1h15'42.4	19	257		
	201	Katayama, Terada, Yorino	Mazda 757	2h39'53.2	34	460		
	62	Dumfries, Ganassi, Thackwell	Kouros Mercedes	2h26'53.8	37	501		
	37	Needell, Sekiya, Hoshino	Toyota 87 C	4h27'23.5	39	528		
	2	Larrauri, Pareja, Schafer	Porsche 962 C	2h37'24.6	40	541		
	29	Olofsson, Ferte, Gonin	Nissan R 86 V	6h06'35.4	86	1164		
	1	Trolle, Belmondo, De Thoisy	Porsche 962 C	6h33'05.4	88	1191		
	15	Palmer, Weaver, Cobb	Porsche 962 C	7h23'47.6	112	1516		
	32	Hasemi, Wada, Suzuki	Nissan R87E	13h54'58.1	117	1584		
	3	Adam, Spenard, Goodyear	Porsche 962 C	8h54'48.2	120	1624		
	61	Thackwell, Pescarolo, Okada	Kouros Mercedes	12h27'39.3	123	1665		
	101	Wilds, Delano, Petery	Ecosse C 286	11h06'20.0	135	1827		
	198	Allison, Andrews, Peters	Tiga GC 286	12h46'18.2	139	1881		
	5	Lammers, Watson, Percy	Jaguar XJR-8	10h40'01.5	158	2139		
	125	Justice, Oudet, Sotty	Tiga GC 85	15h20'39.3	164	2220		
	23	Hoshino, Takahashi, Matsumoto	Nissan R87E	14h48'40.4	181	2450		
	203	Metge, Haldi, Nierop	Porsche 961	16h45'00.6	199	2693		
	6	Brundle, Nielsen, Hahne	Jaguar XJR-8	15h47'54.9	231	3127		

RESULTS AT 4.00 pm SUNDAY

	No.	Drivers	Marques	Hours	Laps	Kms	Average	Group
1.	17	Stuck, Bell, Holbert	Porsche 962 C	23h59'51.1	354	4791	199.661	C1
2.	72	Lassig, Yver, De Dryver	Porsche 962 C	23h55'57.5	334	4521	188.892	C1
3.	13	Raphanel, Courage, Regout	Cougar Porsche	23h55'57.1	331	4480	187.196	C1
4.	11	Fouche, Konrad, Taylor	Porsche 962 C	23h55'58.1	326	4412	184.366	C1
5.	4	Cheever, Boesel	Jaguar XJR-8 LM	23h56'56.6	324	4385	183.111	C1
6.	111	Spice, Velez, De Henning	Spice Pontiac Fiero	23h59'30.7	320	4331	180.527	C2
7.	202	Kennedy, Galvin, Dieudonne	Mazda 757	23h59'38.6	318	4304	179.383	IM
8.	102	Leslie, Mallock, Duez	Ecosse CC 286	23h55'24.1	307	4155	173.689	C2
9.	121	Wood, Los, Hessert	Tiga GC 287	23h59'31.7	274	3709	154.575	C2
10.	114	Thyrring, Sheldon, Harrower	Tiga GC 287	23h59'32.8	271	3668	152.880	C2
11.	177	Heuclin, Lacaud, Descartes	Ald 03	23h56'59.4	269	3641	152.022	C2
12.	40	Grand, Rahier, Terrien	Rondeau 482	23h59'56.5	259	3506	146.071	C1
13.	108	Yvon, Hervalet, Bourjade	Sauber S.H.S.C6	23h00'17.7	257	3478	151.206	C2
14.	127	Adams, Duxbury, Jones	Spice Pontiac Fiero	23h56'57.4	239	3235	135.071	C2
15.	178	Lateste, Tremblay, Boulay	Ald 02	23h57'00.1	235	3181	132.806	C2
		Best lap						
	62	Dumfries, Ganassi, Thackwell	Kouros Mercedes	3'25.4	24		237.224	
		Retired						
	7	Van der Merve, Hobbs, Robinson	Porsche 962 C	0h19'04.8	4	54		
	42	Lombardi, Lempereur, Guillot	Sauber C8	0h18'42.2	4	54		
	117	Schanche, Hoy, Smith	Argo JM 19	0h24'42.7	5	68		
	10	Nissen, Weidler, Takahashi	Porsche 962 C	0h25'48.7	6	81		
	8	Jellinski, Dickens, Haywood	Porsche 962 C	0h29'35.3	7	95		
	200	Fritsch, Pilette, Libert	Argo JM 19	0h54'58.8	12	162		
	118	Iacobelli, Ricci, Tessier	Royale RP40	3h54'32.4	13	176		
	52	Dorchy, Gache, Delestre	WM P 87	3h16'58.3	13	176		
	51	Raulet, Migault, Pessiot	WM P 86	1h02'20.4	14	189		
	18	Wollek, Mass, Schuppan	Porsche 962 C	1h00'49.1	16	217		
	113	Thibault, Heinrich	Chevron	2h48'41.8	18	244		
	36	Jones, Lees, Elgh	Toyota 87 C	1h15'42.4	19	257		
	201	Katayama, Terada, Yorino	Mazda 757	2h35'53.2	34	460		
	62	Dumfries, Ganassi, Thackwell	Kouros Mercedes	2h26'53.8	37	501		
	37	Needell, Sekiya, Hoshino	Toyota 87 C	4h27'23.5	39	528		
	2	Larrauri, Pareja, Schafer	Porsche 962 C	2h37'24.6	40	541		
	29	Olofsson, Ferte, Gonin	Nissan R 86 V	6h06'35.4	86	1164		
	1	Trolle, Belmondo, De Thoisy	Porsche 962 C	6h33'05.4	88	1191		
	15	Palmer, Weaver, Cobb	Porsche 962 C	7h23'47.6	112	1516		
	32	Hasemi, Wada, Suzuki	Nissan R 87 E	13h54'58.1	117	1584		
	3	Adam, Spenard, Goodyear	Porsche 962 C	8h54'48.2	120	1624		
	61	Thackwell, Pescarolo, Okada	Kouros Mercedes	12h27'39.3	123	1665		
	101	Wilds, Delano, Petry	Ecosse C 286	11h06'20.0	135	1827		
	198	Allison, Andrews, Peters	Tiga GC 286	12h46'18.2	139	1881		
	5	Lammers, Watson, Percy	Jaguar XJR-8 LM	10h40'01.5	158	2139		
	125	Justice, Oudet, Sotty	Tiga GC 85	15h20'39.3	164	2220		
	103	Lee Davey, Donovan, Boutinaud	Bardon DB2	15h59'21.2	172	2328		
	23	Hoshino, Takahashi, Matsumoto	Nissan R 87 E	14h48'40.4	181	2450		
	203	Metge, Haldi, Nierop	Porsche 961	16h45'00.6	199	2693		
	116	Taverna, Clements, Trucco	Alba AR3	21h19'54.7	219	2964		
	123	Cooper, Dodd-Noble, Cohen-Olivar	Tiga GC 287	18h01'57.9	224	3032		
	6	Brundle, Nielsen, Hahne	Jaguar XJR-8 LM	15h47'54.9	231	3127		
	181	Crang, Krucker, Bain	Tiga GC 287	21h24'23.9	260	3519		

CLASSIFICATION BY GROUPS

	No.	Entrants	Drivers	Marques	Cyl	Laps	Kms	Average	Group
1.	17	Porsche AG	Stuck, Bell, Holbert	Porsche 962 C	4193	345	4791.777	199.657	C1
2.	72	Primagaz Competition	Lassig, Yver, De Dryver	Porsche 962 C	3920	334	4531.992	188.833	C1
3.	13	Primagaz Competition	Raphanel, Courage, Regout	Cougar Porsche	3920	331	4491.417	187.142	C1
4.	11	Porsche Kremer Racing	Fouche, Konrad, Taylor	Porsche 962 C	3920	326	4425.169	184.382	C1
5.	4	Silk Cut Jaguar	Cheever, Boesel	Jaguar XJR-8	6900	324	4394.891	183.120	C1
6.	202	Mazda Speed Co. Ltd.	Kennedy, Galvin, Dieudonne	Mazda 757	3532	318	4305.037	179.376	IM
7.	40	Graff Racing	Grand, Rahier, Terrien	Rondeau 482	3298	259	3505.718	146.071	C1
1.	111	Spice Engineering Ltd.	Spice, Velez, De Henning	Spice Pontiac Fiero	3300	320	4332.470	180.519	C2
2.	102	Swiftair/Ecurie Ecosse	Leslie, Mallock, Duez	Ecosse C 286	3300	307	4168.510	173.687	C
3.	121	Cosmick/G.P. Motorsport	Wood, Los, Hessert	Tiga GC 287	3300	274	3709.804	154.575	C2
4.	114	Tiga Ford DK	Thyrring, Sheldon, Harrower	Tiga GC 287	3224	271	3669.134	152.880	C2
5.	177	Louis Descartes	Heuclin, Lacaud, Descartes	Ald 03	3453	269	3648.166	152.006	C2

Dave Cundy: 1, 4/5, 10, 11, 12/13, 14/15, 19 (btm right), 20/21, 23, 24, 31, 33, 34 (btm two), 35 (top two), 36 (top), 37 (top right), 38 (top, btm right), 39 (btm right), 40 (btm two), 42 (top right & btm), 43 (top, btm right), 44, 46, 47 (top right), 48, 50/51, 52, 53, 55, 56 (btm), 57 (top), 58 (top), 59 (btm), 60/61, 62, 63, 64/65, 66, 67, 68, 69, 70, 71, 72, 73, 74, 75, 79 (btm), 80, 81 (btm), 82, 83, 86, 87, 88, 89, 90/91, 91, 92, 93, 95, 98/99, 100, 102, 105, 113, 114, 115, 116, 117.

Ken Wells: 2/3, 6, 7, 19 (left, top right), 25, 26/27, 34 (top three), 35 (btm two), 36 (btm two), 37 (top left, btm), 38 (btm left), 39 (top, btm left), 40 (top two), 41 (top), 42 (top left), 43 (btm left), 45, 47 (top left, btm), 54, 56 (top), 56/57, 57 (btm), 58 (btm), 59 (top two), 78, 79 (top centre), 84, 85, 90 (left, top right), 96 (btm two), 101 (btm), 102/103, 104, 106.

Gordon Dawkins: 14, 15, 76/77.

CSS: 16/17.

Steve Payne: 41 (btm).

C. Rietveld: 81 (top), 94, 96 (top).

Another Kimberley publication that might be of interest is:

The Cars of Le Mans – 1987 – a detailed car by car specification.

Please write to:
William Kimberley Limited, 4 Church Close, London, N20 0JU for more details.

FREELANCE JOURNALISM – PHOTOGRAPHY – SPONSOR SERVICES

contact

KEN WELLS
alias The Prancing Tortoise
4 Highfield Rise, Althorne, Essex CM3 6DN
Telephone: **Maldon (0621) 741153 anytime**

DAVID CUNDY
alias The Happy Snapper
24 Victoria Drive, Leigh on Sea, Essex SS9 1SF
Telephone: **Southend (0702) 711330 evenings**

All photographs in this book were taken on Fuji Film

All photographs in this book were taken on Fuji Film

120